GOD'S
SMUGGLER,
JR.

God has an Exciting Life for You!

COPYRIGHT PAGE

Cover Design: Marcus Stallworth
Photographer Back Cover: Rachel D. Koontz
Photographer on Flaps: Donna Crow, Mary Ann Tan, ARS
Photography design: Sandi Chai Brown, Tim Dees,
Christopher Gaston
Endless Editors: I'm deeply grateful for your help

Clip Art acknowledgement:
The images used herein were obtained from Corel Clipart, ©
Corel Corporation 1998 and its subsidiary
es, 1600 Carling Ave., Ottawa, Ontario, Canada K1Z 8R7

Scripture taken from the Holy Bible, New International Version (NIV)

Copyright 1973, 1978, 1984

Scripture taken from the NEW AMERICAN STANDARD BIBLE

Copyright 1960, 1962, 1963, 1968, 1971, 1972, 1973, 1975, 1977

by The Lockman Foundation (www.Lockman.org)

ISBN: **978-0892281626**

Additional copies may be ordered:
www.peggyjoyceruth.org
www.crosslines.net

CONTENTS

ACKNOWLEDGEMENTS

To Glenda Huff, who was the first to say,
"Angie you need to write a book!"

To my Mother, Peggy Joyce, who I thought was
crazy when she said,
"Angie you have to write a book three times
before it will be ready,"
Two years later,
it was a gross understatement.
Truly, I think this book would have been handed
back and forth from proofer to proofer endlessly
if I had not put a stop to it
& put in footnote 48!
Mom, thanks for cheering me on!

To Donna, who wished she had written the book so
she could tell her side of it first.
She really helped give new meaning to
"partners in crime".
Thanks for what you taught me on the trip
of a lifetime!

FOREWORD

A NGELIA AND I BECAME friends in college for two reasons, we both loved God like crazy and we were both adventure seekers.

Angelia would always intrigue me with wild tales of her exploits for God and I had a few of my own to tell. It was so great to find someone who was as hungry and in love with Jesus as I was and who wasn't afraid of jumping out on a limb to see what God just might do!

Years have passed since those college days, and Angelia has never wavered in her passion for Jesus and her zeal to be right in the middle of God's great adventure to snatch up lives for His Kingdom. She's dedicated her blood, sweat and tears to reach this next generation, and I love her for it!!

A few weeks ago Angie sent me this manuscript and asked me to write a foreword. I didn't have time, but when I picked it up to read it, once again her amazing stories drew me in and I couldn't put it down!

You will love this book and Angelia—she's hilarious and real and full of faith in God. Her life will challenge you to live an extra-ordinary life of your own. She'll encourage you to climb out on that limb, trusting and believing God for yourself to see what God just might possibly do through you!

Katie Luce
Teen Mania Ministries

MISSION TEAM INFORMATION

If a student desires to join a mission trip, I highly recommend these two possibilities... I participated in a Teen Mania mission trip with a team of 14 high school students from our youth group. Teen Mania has outreaches all around the globe. Crosslines College Ministries trains students from Howard Payne University to evangelize, serve and minister on mission teams who travel all over the world. I highly recommend Howard Payne University for furthering your academic education and would encourage a youth to be an active part of the verse in Matthew 24: 14 in which Jesus states: "And this gospel of the kingdom shall be preached in the whole world for a witness to all the nations, and then the end shall come."   www.crosslines.net

Team Mania Ministries takes youth on overseas missions as well as producing the "Acquire the Fire" regional youth conventions. Acquire the Fire features musical acts, speakers and more. Global Expeditions is a ministry of TMM leading teenagers from across North America taking the message of Jesus Christ to the nations. The Honor Academy is designed to cultivate and develop the leadership potential in young adults while preparing them to impact today's world for Christ.
www.teenmania.org   http://www.honoracademy.com

Howard Payne University is a private university affiliated with the Baptist General Convention of Texas. Located in Brownwood, Texas, the university has more than fifty majors, minors and pre-professional programs within the schools of science and math, business, Christian studies, education, music and fine arts, and humanities.   The university was recognized in the 2005 and 2006 editions of "America's Best Colleges" published by *U.S. News & World Report*. The Douglas MacArthur Academy of Freedom is a unique multidisciplinary honors program designed to instill leadership quality in students seeking to further their education after college or enrich their undergraduate degree.

www.hputx.edu

PREFACE

ACLOSE FRIEND OF my mom once invited our family to her home for an evening to dine over a meal with many courses. She explained that the *experience* would take several hours and asked that we allow enough time and not ruin it by rushing. She explained, "Some people *eat* meals, but others, *dine.*" In this recount of smuggling Bibles into a foreign, exotic land, the reader has a choice to hurriedly get to the focal point of the book or take time to dine. I'm inviting you to *go with us* as I retell every step of the way on this adventure. My personal challenge to you, the reader, is to escape boredom and come out from among the empty. Live a life with impact, and let God put together a personalized adventure all your own.

To avoid a theme in the opening pages would be to reduce this account to mere journal notes of a number of countries. The bulk of the book takes place in a time span of three weeks; the highpoint occurred in a span of less than twenty-four hours, but the changing of the heart was done country by county. The trip itinerary began in Taiwan, moved to the Philippines, and on to Hong Kong. These events came two weeks before we even began the smuggling in China. The team ended in Japan, which was the place of our goodbyes. There is no point in spoiling the experience by rushing to the last chapters to deliver up the action which has been promised. Names, dates and specific pinpointed locations have been avoided for obvious reasons.

The *introduction* lunges ahead in time, by dropping you, the reader, in the middle of a Texas Youth Commission facility and into public classrooms where my smuggling adventure circulates before I ever arrive and stirs imaginations long after I leave. The power of a person's testimony often emits a lingering effect long after that person's name is forgotten. However, I didn't always have a story and it is a good thing for me to remember, for it is a pitiful, helpless feeling to have nothing interesting about your life and to have the consequent problem that it causes when it's your turn next to speak. There was a time I opened my mouth and God hadn't yet filled it. Once I asked, it took only one week for God to bring something to pass that would forever alter my life. *How life has always been is not necessarily how life will always be. And that can be the good news.* A pivotal realization of personal emptiness and anecdote, which took place on that first trip in a poverty-stricken area of the Philippines concludes the *introduction* and is the backdrop for the rest of the book.

Invited by a friend, to share this smuggling adventure with youth in San Antonio, I especially enjoy the interaction time afterwards. Perhaps, it is because the pressure is released you actually feel the drop. But as I left, the internal spigot never shut down. I threw my speaking notes on the seat of the car and jumped in. Immediately, something inside knew it was time to commit the story to paper, and the chapters began to outline as quickly as I could scribble them on a scrap napkin. After years of sharing this adventure, it took less than a month to record it on paper. However, when I went back and read the narrative to myself, I noticed two things. First, I could see how God went to work immediately on requests I had made randomly through my life and it required my reading it myself to realize how many layers of details and non-arbitrary actions from everyone involved had gone into His handiwork. Understanding came to me in layers. Secondly, I realized I had told it through the eyes and from the perspective of the age I was when I experienced it. Actually, the story told itself from the viewpoint of the self-focused child to the raw, green teenager with whatever traces of adult imagery you might detect sprinkled within. Remember, it is just a viewpoint from earth—whether it is either a 48" or a 68" viewpoint makes little difference when it only serves to tell a story, which describes something much greater. So let me be the first to recommend the story of this adventure, for each time I have read these pages I have learned more about the God I serve, His creativity, His genius of planning the details of our life and His ever-abounding sense of humor.

INTRODUCTION: Never Again!

THE SECURITY CAMERA WAS pointing directly at me. Twenty-nine out of the thirty young men in bright orange uniforms were listening attentively to the Monday night lesson. It was a battle of wills; with one teenage boy determined to get the better of me. Tonight I was testing the new empathy concept, which theorizes that the *more* you know a person, the *less likely* you are to commit a crime against that person. I like to believe these young men would never consider harming me if given the chance. In this room were some of the state's most aggressive teenage offenders. They had shared with me horrible stories from their criminal pasts, ranging from aggravated violence to sexual assault of children.

This cantankerous young man, however, openly splintered that theory when he interjected, "Miss, if you were *my next door* neighbor, *I'd rob ya!*" Laughter erupted in the group. I, too, snickered under my breath at how far the two of us had yet to go. If the commotion continued and I didn't regain command, he would be expelled by the alerted staff. We were instructed in Education 101 at college that in public school settings, one should move into the proximity of a disruptive student and gently place a hand on the shoulder to subtly refocus attention. Instead, I slammed the hard heel of my thick-soled shoe to the floor and gave the camera monitor a quick, disarming smile... With artistic, comic timing, the young man let out a howl, pretending I had come in contact with his foot, which was only protected by a flimsy, open-toed cloth house-slipper. Now, having regained complete attention, I expounded my own rendition of the familiar verse for the guys to commit to memory, "It is much better to enter heaven with five *broken* toes, than to enter hell with all *good* ones!"

The boy's face grimaced with animated pain as he endeavored with much drama to use both hands to act as though he was having to pull his foot loose from some unseen clamp. Delighted howls pealed out from the regulars, who were well acquainted with the nightly antics my dad and I had employed for years to capture the attention of these tough young men. I pulled back to the lesson for the remaining time I had left, and slipped into my testimony of **"a tale of smugglers on a dark night in a far away land... loaded down with laundry bags... running down an alley with a thousand eyes..."**

What would make guys who had committed horrible crimes listen to a white girl who had never smoked a cigarette or drank a beer? My credentials didn't seem to be the proper background match for effective prison ministry, especially to youth who weren't *prone to listening* anyway.

Since college I have recruited every known friend to volunteer at the Texas Youth Commission on Monday nights. Each week all eleven dorms have volunteers in place and afterwards we meet in the guardhouse to swap stories.[1]

The beauty of working with one of these forgotten young people is if one of them truly changes, then his life, his family and his children will have a radically different outcome. A second benefit occurred to me after a conversation I had with several recently incarcerated young men. I remember mentioning a certain neighborhood in San Antonio where I had friends and from memory these youth could map out the homes in which they planned to strike. My friends did not know I was doing them a favor by weekly volunteering with the ones who raided their section of town. Each criminal leaves an enormous trail of heartache and trouble. More importantly, when a man's heart changes, any future victims are protected and will never know what one volunteer did to prevent upcoming tragedy from striking them.

---

[1] When I began at TYC, I was a teenager and younger than some of the offenders with whom I was working. I was determined to develop a new program for these youthful offenders, but the volunteer coordinator lamented: **"You are going to get stabbed and ruin my program..."** After her retirement, we crossed paths again, and I greeted her with, "Nancy, I'm still at it, and I never got stabbed." We both had a good laugh.

Never has any of the one hour volunteer sessions with these incarcerated youth produced a less-than-eventful evening for us. Sometimes we had a doubter, or better said, a heckler, in the crowd but God had a special knack for confirming my stories in a very dramatic, unforgettable way. Soon after I had returned from China, my smuggling companion became my partner at Hope Dorm for Monday night Bible study. This group of young men was absorbing every lesson and I had grown quite attached to them. The staff would let us hold our group in the back kitchen for the sake of helping the young men concentrate and to minimize interruptions; I, for one, enjoyed the added privacy. One boy routinely set an eraser in the self-locking door so we would not have to stop and get staff to unlock the door every time a youth wanted to join the Bible lesson. Tonight my cup overflowed with enthusiastic listeners, and chairs were jammed tightly together in the undersized space. When I introduced my China cohort, the regulars begged me to tell more of our smuggling story. My partner was constantly moving into the exit hallway to avoid group interruptions because the boys yearned for individual prayer for personal challenges and family troubles.

I was deeply into the story of the two of us lugging suitcases full of Bibles when I casually mentioned, "All it would have taken was *one phone call* to the Chinese authorities from anyone in that dark alley saying we looked suspicious, and we were *busted.*"

Immediately the boys exploded with questions. Hands waved wildly in front of my face, begging me to call on them. I yielded the floor to one of our regulars. "How did God keep you from getting caught?" he asked excitedly. The question caught me off-guard since I had never really answered that for myself. I replied off the cuff, "Maybe angels...? With that many people in the alley, the only explanation that I can think of is God must have made us invisible that night."

"I don't believe you!" challenged a new guy. I had never seen this young man before; but occasionally, I ran across a kid with a lot of attitude. "He's a Satanist, don't listen to him. Go on!" demanded another guy to my right. Suddenly, the situation shifted to something I had never experienced. The new guy seemed very agitated and drew back his fist and hissed, "I don't believe you! Let's see what angels you have protecting you now!" and with the force of a hammer, he slammed forward...

I hadn't eaten all day and didn't have much fight in me. I wish I could report something noble or spiritual here, but it happened so fast and the last conscious thought which went through my head was "Oh my, I feel weak!" as I braced for the impact. I opened my eyes when I heard him scream. Someone, next to the door, yelled for staff assistance. Minutes later when security arrived, the boy was still lying on the floor with his legs drawn up to his chest. He gave the impression of someone who was coming cold turkey off a drug high; his body trembled in convulsions and his speech was slurred except for splattered cursing. One of the security men asked me how this happened, and I honestly replied, "I'm not sure, sir. This boy was causing a disruption and the next thing I knew he ended up sprawled on the floor." When the staff left, the boys were horrified they had not attempted to stop this young man; yet it was obvious, I hadn't needed their protection. Like boys do, they talked over each other, telling *their* rendition of the night's events.

The last picture in my mind was the young man's clenched hand slamming forward toward me... Yet in full-force motion, his fist suddenly stopped as if it had hit an invisible barrier within a hair's-breath of direct contact with my face. The young men recounted this story over and over—rapidly repeating my last words: *angels had protected us and* then demonstrating the guy's fist stopping a fraction of an inch from my face. Each was telling his version of what he had witnessed with his own eyes. More than thirty boys witnessed it; *but not my smuggling partner,* she was around the corner praying with two guys; *and not me,* I had my eyes closed!

Years of volunteering has yielded a variety of special memories and occasionally these guys, in their own unique way, let a volunteer know he is appreciated... Several guys in orange prison jumpsuits involuntarily ducked as something LARGE abruptly flew over us. The art and refinement of acceptable expression has not been perfected by this group of young ruffians and certain events can trigger some unexpected flare-ups. A chair had sailed over our heads and crashed, slamming full-force into the wall. Immediately staff restrained the young man and pinned him on the floor to prevent any further incidents.

Before policy changes from the Texas Governor made our Monday night program at the juvenile correctional institution a religious *right* rather than a *privilege*[2], staff would occasionally order a young man's removal from the hour-long lessons as common leverage for various offenses during the week. Many of them deserved to be removed for their disruptions; however, before this law, occasionally, it was undue. Numerous times the removal—of both those I was thankful for and those I regretted—escalated into a full blown incident as the young offender would begin to argue and curse and swear threats of violence towards the antagonist in an attempt to stay for the rest of the story. Security would rush in, put an end to the disturbance and carry the youth to

---

[2] George W. Bush signed into effect GAP law 91.21 stating "TYC shall encourage the participation of volunteer religious groups and individuals in its religious services and programs." That law directly related to our program. I once had the opportunity to thank him personally for the major difference this legislation made. Bible study privileges being taken away is only a deterrent with church choir boys. TYC staff is very supportive of this concept and now they steer the very worst offenders toward us each week.

security cells to *cool off.* Some became belligerent, but I'm still haunted by the ones who cried out to me for help. Despite their pitiful pleas, all I could do was continue the lesson with those remaining.

This particular night the young man had been hanging onto every word and was yanked up unexpectedly. He was denied when he pled to stay and begged for mercy. "I want to hear the end of the story!" and with that, he punctuated his sentence with the flying chair. I shall never forget the look of confusion, etched with desperation, in the young boy's face as he turned, handcuffed and subdued, to look me directly in the eyes *as if* to ask me why I wasn't coming to his rescue.

~

There wasn't a stark difference I could distinguish between the youth in this prison setting and that of the high school classroom where I had applied for a job as a substitute teacher. The weekly practice of group instruction at the TYC definitely prepared me for the next assignment of handling the rowdy youth of a resource class in the public school.

"The last substitute left in tears when the students set off fireworks in the back of the classroom," the high school principal diplomatically explained to me as I accepted the offer of substitute teacher in one of their more challenging programs. Briefing me on the history of the kids in this particular class, he asked me warily, "Are you up to the task?" I was fresh out of college; he and I were both worried I would be a soft touch and, worse yet, an easy target.

I knew what I was in for, my memory wasn't that short. Back during my high school days, I remembered how we had tormented the young substitute by having the whole class face backwards, including reversing her desk and chair. She broke under our first assault. Now, I was clearly the one on trial. I knew I deserved everything I would get that first day, so I cleared my throat and dove in: *"If every student will do his work and put it on my desk, then I will spend the last ten minutes before the bell rings telling how I was part of a smuggling operation in China."* The lethargic mood abruptly shifted.

The teachers for whom I substituted were perplexed. Upon their return, they would invariably ask me, "How is it that you are the only substitute teacher who manages to get these students to do their work?" I would accept it as a compliment and offer a friendly, *"It's my little secret,"* thus bringing the conversation to an end and avoiding any extra scrutiny. In two years' time I never received a reprimand or even the slightest word of disapproval. All I experienced were hungry youth.

As I passed through the high school cafeteria trying to locate the classroom where I was scheduled to sub, a rousing cheer burst out, *"We want Miss Ruth! We want Miss Ruth!"* The high school students banged their silverware in unison on the tables. I scurried to my next class, half-awed that they actually liked being witnessed to, and nervous that if a seasoned teacher heard the commotion, they would suspect that my appeal was due to inexperience or leniency.

A couple of veteran teachers ganged up on me in the teacher's lounge, "Substituting is like babysitting; how are you doing it? You're able to get actual class work out of these students." I'm sure I struck them as a *pushover.* I responded back, "It's a secret you *don't want* to know!" I figured it was only a matter of time before some student would accidentally spill the beans, but to my knowledge, the students guarded our adventures as much as if they had been *with me* in China.

One student stands out in my mind, as she would beg me to share more adventures in exchange for encouraging each student to complete the work assigned. She even attempted to reschedule her friends to be placed in my classes. I was amazed that some of the other teachers gave permission for their students to be our "extra visitors." (One teacher doubled the size of one of my classes instantly when she dumped *her* entire class on *mine* and left.) This particular young girl assumed the task of becoming *my personal manager* and inciting the students to beg for certain stories. Like a child who hurries to wash the dishes so they can get outside to play, she took it upon herself to meet my one requirement: to make sure all the class work was in a folder on my desk so we could have our *play* time.

What made the biggest impression on me was how she would listen with such enthusiasm— like she was hearing each story for the first time. If I abbreviated a story for the sake of time, she would raise her hand and remind me of the infraction. Trying to keep it interesting for her, since she had heard my narratives so many times, I began to research my old journals for any scraps of information from my adventures overseas. She reveled in each new detail.

There were times I felt like these youth knew me better than my own family and my closest friends. Questions took on a personal nature: *Did you always want to smuggle? Were you afraid? How did you become a smuggler? Were you breaking the law? What would have happened if you had been captured?*

Questions were answered in earnest and a heartfelt rapport developed between me and each class. I can't say that what I did was easy since as far back as I could remember I had a deep aversion to public speaking; but I didn't want a student walking out of class thinking about my life but contemplating his own. A direct invitation to personally respond insured that the story was not shared for sheer entertainment value, but to make a personal investment into the life of each of the students.

The promised ten-minute thriller tale of illegal smuggling in a dark land always had a bold personal challenge attached at the end: "I *dare* you to serve God! I dare you to NOT waste your life!" As approximately thirty students gave me their undivided attention,[3] I would add in, "Oh yeah, and one more thing. I promise you—*your life will never be boring!*" Until now, I never released my secret for obtaining successful class work![4]

---

[3] Why should we be afraid to be bold in the public school system? What were they going to do if they caught me – cut my tongue out? Torture me? If I had risked my life in Communist China for people to have the gospel, the price of freedom of speech in America is ridiculously petty by comparison. Too many people shy away from sharing open testimonies in the classroom. Sadly, for the majority of Americans, it only takes the threat of a monetary blow to our pocketbooks to silence our witness to the next generation.

[4] When I come in contact with youth, something ignites inside me; I cannot stand to see youth *waste* their lives. I not only survived two years in public education but gathered from it some of the best experiences of my life; only because I shared my experiences with them. Contrary to what most adults think, young people are hungry for something that has substance.

Eagerness and enthusiasm reached new levels when the students begged me to come to their churches to meet their pastors, and homes to visit with their families. *"Why has no one ever told me this before?" "I wish you were my Sunday School teacher!" "You make me want to serve God more than my pastor!" "You should be on the radio!"* Chants for added time for more stories and appeals begging for future classes resounded as I shut the door and left for home. Finished work was neatly piled on my desk and imaginations had been ignited in the hearts of bored youth.

~

Reminiscing through my journals I need to go back now to where it started. It was on that very first mission trip to the Far East when I initially spotted the same type of starvation in myself as I was seeing in many of these TYC and high school students. Youth seem to hunger for something they can't quite determine or define. In the Philippines, I remember sitting in a circle with some of the poorest people on earth when I first came face to face with that culprit of just how ordinary my life was at that point.

Hungry Filipino faces were staring at me and I was panicking. It was that thing in life I dreaded the most—public speaking. You probably know the feeling you get in your stomach when everyone has to make an oral presentation, and you know you're next. *What on earth could I share about my life that would have any positive effect on them?* My life was ordinary and their life was horrifying. I can't even begin to describe the living conditions in Manila's squatter areas. I had never seen real poverty before this. Their huts were made of cardboard and sheets of tin. Broken glass littered the ground under my feet, and the air and water was filled with the stench of animal and human waste. Everyone had to give a testimony, and I was terrified—*"I don't have one word to say to these people that will make any difference in their lives."*

Red was creeping up my neck and over my face as my turn to speak approached. I had never given my testimony and this was my first realization that I had very little to contribute. I didn't have a great testimony like I had admired in so many—the *"I got delivered from…"* to capture people's interest. I remember the sweat on my palms and my hands turning cold.

Can you relate to that feeling? Perhaps you lived in a sheltered home, and you can't think of what to share. Or maybe what you did was so bad you can't share it. Or your story simply has nothing to connect with in these people. I had traveled all the way over here and realized I didn't have anything to impart. Our American testimonies tend to sound like the filler we use in our English papers when we don't know what to say—a bunch of spiritual sounding jargon to fill up the space. Immediately I was dismayed by the $2700 this trip had cost, and I wondered if we would have done better to let them share their testimonies with us.

I pushed as hard as I could, trying to get something to come up. My brain and my heart physically hurt from the internal pressure I was putting on my memory file. I had reached an invisible, internal marker—for the first time, I faced my own emptiness.

Since I had nothing from my personal life to relate, I did the only thing I could think to do; I slipped in my mother's testimony of being delivered after eight years of emotional sickness. Hopefully, it helped them more than I thought, but the impact of my words seemed hollow. As the interpreter finished translating, I made a vow to myself, *"NEVER AGAIN, will I ever substitute someone else's testimony for mine."*

If I were to summarize the one theme that characterizes my life, it would be—*God has an exciting life designed for you. It is a sin to live a boring life. There is something drastically wrong if serving GOD is not fun!*

The most damaging thing in youth work is for an individual to relate his testimony in a superficial way. It is apparent when someone attempts to add spirituality to their message by using that little Shakespearean voice while reading a verse—acting like God is a distant third party and treating the scripture like a boring midday college lecture! What a disservice that is to those students, especially prisoners, who aren't listening to *what* is being said, but *how* it is being said. If the person reading scripture is inwardly bored, it comes across loud and clear just as the youth suspected: "Christianity IS boring.[5]" Every time I speak, I hope *boredom* falls, just assuredly as the total collapse of the walls of Jericho and East Berlin.

I have shared this smuggling story hundreds of times but it still impacts me personally each time—that God has rescued my life from **ordinary.** I was born in an unheard of place, endowed with average intelligence, and had little in the way of worldly goods; added to that was a distinct speech impediment, innate shyness and little personal ambition. Summed up in one person, this left very little chance for anything promising. But God has wrought marvelous things from such a one. God delivers us from a stale, boring life.[6]

---

[5] It looks irreverent to even see the words *boring* and *Christianity* in the same sentence.

[6] Peter also targets emptiness in **1 Peter 1:18,** ...you were redeemed from the empty way of life handed down to you from your forefathers." NIV

Whatever is boring about your life is *backslidden* and *unredeemed!* I personally believe that emptiness is the one thing people fear the most. From my earliest remembrances I recall hating that empty feeling. I start to feel a panic that my life is wasting and I'm losing time if I watch a movie that lacks real substance. Boring, shallow conversations at parties unnerve me because of the cheap empty feeling it leaves inside of me. Sadly, people learn to cope with that emptiness feeling in all kinds of ways—instead of being *delivered* from it.

Stop and take an inventory of your life…
Ask yourself: *"Is my life boring?"*
"Do I have an empty life?"
Search for areas that are boring in your life
and see if God is in those areas.

That experience in the squatter area in the Philippines would be the last time I lived off of someone else's walk with God. Actually, that is what growing up is all about. I had cut the apron strings and let go of the coattails. For the first time I was owning my own faith. My insides were screaming—*"GOD, are you with me?"* I really didn't know.

From the moment I made that decision, sitting in front of those cardboard houses, it took only ONE week for God to give me a testimony that would forever change my life. And this is that story… (*Well, let me back up a little…*)

CHAPTER ONE
Be Careful of the Prayers You Pray!

I REMEMBER BEING PERSUADED to leave for G. A. camp as a nine or ten-year-old. At night, the crying started in pitiful waves. I would lie in bed and the walls themselves seemed to wail. The sounds of muffled cries in the night gave us the creeps as mournful serenades of sobbing in pillows came from the dark shadows of the barracks. It was horrible. It gave us a case of homesickness that we would never forget.

I have a theory that the basis of most of one's carnal knowledge comes from these camps. It is amazing that my first visual encounter with the occult came not from movies, television or slumber parties, but from children of church people. You have all these distorted people together sharing information, and we call it *church camp.*[7] When they began to successfully levitate other campers, I moved away from *that* group and toward the group in the corner who had the experts at the magic card-tricks. (I might be forced to join Rushdie if I published a handbook on *What I Learned At Church Camp!*)

---

[7] These are not my views now; at this time I was part of the problem they had. Also, since the advent of Youth Pastors and Youth Groups, church camps have drastically improved in my opinion. No longer do adults use them as a summer babysitting week, but campers come home with their lives impacted and changed.

Nonetheless, I am still prolific at the card tricks, especially the one called *cops and robbers.*

I guess we were all too young to be at camp, *or* there was just a cloud of depression over this group, *or* perhaps we had conjured up something. The whole barrack seeped with melancholy. We felt engulfed and trapped with nothing productive to do, so the sponsors decided to try something fresh. Attempting to break up the monotony, they began reading books to us, like children in story hour. It strikes me as ironic that people can feel desperately homesick for a home that has its problems, too.

My family was going through some hard times—my mom was in the turmoil of what had been eight years of emotional trouble. Even with shock treatments and psychiatrists, her condition had grown steadily worse. My dad escaped into his work. We had many family issues. My life was an absolute mess and shadows of empty darkness had squeezed into my soul. I was a boring, selfish, timid little character.

At this camp I thought like I was an outsider peering in on life, but not really participating. I was very much a gnarled ball of yarn, myself, as Corrie Ten Boom says, or rather illustrates, it best. She lifts up her needlework, stretched tightly in the large hoops, displaying countless colored threads running in every direction with tangles of loops and twisted knots. Her stitches were random and disordered with no apparent purpose. She would say, "This is what our life looks like: a confusing, tangled mess." Then she flips her needlework to the front side—revealing an embroidered motif of a beautiful crown: and there is *order*, and *design*, and *purpose*. "This is what God does to the other side of our life, He weaves us for good..."[8] God is always working both sides—but at that point in my life, all I could see were the knots.[9]

The camp counselors, according to their new strategy to end the monotony, called out choices of book titles, one by one. The girl next to me suggested that I link up with her group, but I declined. By this time everyone in the audience had joined a reading group and I was shocked to find I was the only camper left. I was standing alone in the tabernacle because I never made a move. This put me in the final group—by default. The announcer

---

[8] Corrie Ten Boom, a Dutch POW who described her survival Nazi concentration camps in the holocaust of World War II in her book A Prisoner and Yet. *See* Chapter 3: Light through Iron Bars at Vught. Reference also: Genesis 50: 20, Romans 8: 26-28

[9] Knotted lives: One young man ashamedly confessed to me something he had done and it was memorably horrible. He worried if God could ever use him for anything. I replied, "Smile, it will make a great testimony! Youth ministers always seem to have the most notoriously interesting pasts." And as you might suspect, he is now a youth pastor.

pointed toward a lady with a small group gathered around her and told me to go join it.

Like a mother takes out a storybook at bedtime, the lady seated us at her feet and opened the book she had pulled from her purse. This idea was already beginning to spark our cure. From the very first page she read of *God's Smuggler by Brother Andrew,* it opened a brand new world to our minds... This introduction to smuggling not only made me forget my homesickness, but it forever altered my life. I wish I could find that woman and thank her for not only making a temporary difference in my life, but for shaping my future permanently. Christianity in a simple form crystallized upon my soul and captured my interest. Until that point, I had not seen anything worth the commitment. We were hearing tales of a young man who was smuggling Bibles into communist countries and the suspense of missionaries hiding Bibles in the framework of their cars to bypass border checks. Each afternoon I lived for the moment when we would hear the continuation of the story.[10]

I wasn't saved when I was at that camp, nor did I make a commitment to Christ. I've always frozen up

---

[10] One of my proofreaders made a marginal comment here: "Much like your high school students who would hang onto every detail of your story." (p. 19) Live in a way that your life story becomes contagious.

around emotionalism, revolting inwardly against overt displays. At retreats, it was the same pattern—they sat in a circle, strummed the guitar, collectively sang *Kum-ba-ya*, and then attempted to hug you—crying like someone chopping up onions. It was as though the music had to be just right to get you in the mood to handle the duty of such a charitable deed as hugging an undesirable. And it never seemed to me that anyone was any different the next week. Nevertheless, despite my clammed-up attitude and the assessment I had made about what all His people were doing, God was pulling on my heart; in a sacred moment, I knelt at the altar the last day of camp—not to get saved, of course, but to dedicate myself to smuggling. The person designated to pray with me tried to reason me into some other things. But despite the sales pitch for other areas, I already knew what I wanted and I didn't change my position at the altar. On that altar I told God, with whom I wasn't on close terms, "When I grow up, I want to be a Bible smuggler."

I noticed everyone else went forward for more conventional reasons—for *salvation*, or dedicating their lives to be a *Sunday school teacher* or *a pastor's wife* or something as equally unimaginative. *It was truly shocking to me that they could hear such a fabulous story and not be moved.* However, the criticism of my decision did not stop there. The staff was concerned (perhaps they felt guilty about me actually applying something to my life they read to me), and by the time I arrived home, they had called my parents to solicit their aid in getting me to recant. "We feel there is something a little wrong with your kid and we are not sure what it is. She dedicated her life to... (their voices grew incoherent at this point), and we think she's serious." They tried with all the compulsion of a fiery evangelist to persuade me into getting saved. I didn't want to get saved; I explained it to them politely, "I want to smuggle Bibles when I grow up!" So that's how I started out—I wanted to work **for God** before I even **knew Him**.

Years went by and the story resumes around junior high. I was quiet. I wasn't in the popular crowd. There were no youth groups, and I felt like I was on my own. Sitting in my room on the weekends, it felt like the walls were caving in. The emptiness of my life was worse than ever. I wasn't moving in any direction. The people I admired started getting into trouble, but they were also empty—just on a faster track than I was, to nowhere.

Have you ever had the sensation you were facing two roads in life? I could feel the two roads just as surely as if they converged out my front door.

I knew I now had to make a choice. My peers were experimenting with the things most teenagers were drawn to; I could follow them or choose this other *unknown* road on which I saw no other youth traveling.

A few years before, I'd had a mild, seemingly uneventful salvation experience. Typically, every time God confronted my life to get my attention, it was in a dramatic way. However, my salvation experience was not marked by anything memorable. One would think since all of heaven has a great commotion of rejoicing over one lost soul who repents, a little of that explosive celebration would vibrate down to earth. Nothing about the earthly side of the event is impressed upon my mind so for the record, it suffices to say: I made the decision in private, walked the aisle in public and did not hear any of the angels rejoicing as I made the journey down that aisle. The event passed unnoticed on this side of heaven, with not even a notation in the front of our family Bible.

Yet, at this later time, alone in my room—I did experience the vibrations of heaven, and the encounter was stamped upon my soul. I became intensely aware of the presence of God. Something spiritual was clearly wrapped in a very natural impartation of awareness. Instantly, I knew the reason for the moment— God was asking me to make a life choice. He was asking specifically for something from me.

The moment was so strongly emblazoned upon me that I actually felt in a position to make a counter offer. I had a prerequisite for God, so I reciprocated with my own conditions, "God, I'm going to make You a deal. I'll promise You that I'll never get into trouble like the kind these other kids are in, if You will make me a solemn promise my life will never be boring!" In hindsight, I would probably put some stipulations on that agreement.[11]

God's pleasure at what I asked bordered the tangible; it was *as though this Big Hand came down from heaven and we shook on it.* Something significant had taken place. I could feel the excitement of the negotiation and the pact we had made. We both seemed really happy with our agreement. I progressed through school and very little changed outwardly. But God and I had a bargain. So, I didn't get in trouble and I could feel that He had hold of me now.

---

[11] As an adult now some specific *stipulations* come to my mind, since I've found that *not boring* is dangerous left as an open ended request. But God and I made the deal, and He has been faithful to His end of the bargain. I have never had a boring year; then I noticed I never had a boring month, then week, and now, His faithfulness is by the hour.

CHAPTER TWO
Never to be Bored Again!

DONNA WAS CRYING BECAUSE I was *told* to go and had *no desire,* and she had *the desire,* but *not a direct order!* I pieced together broken fragments of how unfair Donna perceived life and noticed that these weren't crocodile tears. I was amused myself at the turn of events and was in a low-grade state of shock over how my life's script appeared pre-written for me and I was just playing the role. I had put very little effort into making it to this meeting and yet, I had become the center of attention. Personally, I had little aspiration in life, so it was ironic I would be chosen and everyone around me would be crying with jealousy. Even though no intention of my own, Donna gave the impression of having a personal conflict with me; and while I barely knew her, what she thought about me *mattered* to me. What made matters worse, it bothered her enough to cry in public. She was fun, popular, and several years older—which made the situation awkward for me on several fronts. Here I was, surrounded by crowds of people asking me questions as if I had any *hand* in why I had been singled out a few minutes before. She felt snubbed by heaven itself, and I felt cornered.

Small decisions can cause such different conclusions. Earlier in the evening I was involved in a hot game of tennis with a fellow church member when I remembered *the meeting,* which had already begun. I first decided to let *whatever my tennis partner wanted to do* determine my course for the evening. He was opposed to getting cleaned up for a service, so he declined. I didn't know why, but I went anyway. I sat in the very back, hair smoothed over, but unshowered and still wearing a sports suit—I came to observe, not to be seen. I had never laid eyes on this woman evangelist, but wanted to hear more about the underground church, then skip out early. The next thing I knew, out of a crowd of a hundred or more, she pointed straight at me and announced, "The Lord has spoken to me that this young girl is suppose to go in five weeks on a crusade to Asia with me."

I froze stiff in my chair; I hated the Orient. (The only thing that perked my interest was *the clandestine aspects* of the adventure—sneaking Bibles into a communist country.) She dramatically announced, "Someone in this audience should pay her way!"

Something in me softened. My uncle moved forward and whispered to this Asian evangelist and she nodded: I sat there startled over how close I had been to not coming and stunned that I was the only person in this meeting commissioned, actually *commanded,* to go on the trip. Small decisions make big differences—all I had done was show up, and **not** dressed for success at that, and here I was, facing China!

Saying the noble thing that one friend would say to another in one of these situations, I vowed to Donna, "I won't go either unless we can raise your money so you can go with me!" I wondered if I would be struck by lightning, since I was pulled out of an audience and *told to go*, a selection that seemed to have been made by a higher source.[12] It gave me a funny feeling after I said it, but she cheered up, and the conflict melted. It proved to be the Lord's plan because the trip honestly took the *combination* of the two of us to make happen what happened. God was in those words I had just spoken.

Not only was I green to traveling, but I was a rookie when it came to missions. I was the naïve and shy one; Donna was the talkative go-getter. She had continuous motion—like she had a treadmill under her feet—and together God used her strength of momentum and my internal compass of right and wrong. "*Innocents Abroad*" might have been the name of this chapter—however, that is someone else's book and probably not too accurate of a description of Donna. ☺

If I had made a list of the top 100 countries I wanted to visit, no country in the Orient would have made the list. However, the descriptions of the

---

[12] I knew enough of my Bible to know there are times that a person can be responsible to God for what someone else tells him. Pilate's wife received for her husband the warning from the dream, not Pilate. (Matthew 27: 19) And Saul seemed to always be in trouble for not doing what Samuel told him 'the Lord was telling him' to do. I Samuel 10: 8; I Samuel 13: 11-14; I Samuel 15: 3, 17-19.

persecuted church and the underground work captured my imagination. Each night I wrestled with confused turmoil over the destination of the trip. In fact, I think it was more than lack of desire; it was the notion that I, at that point and time in life, did not like anything Oriental. I had a distaste for the furniture, the food, and I had a deep-seated repugnance to their gods. My mind could not process exactly what had happened to my family, but I knew, invisible or not—something had wrecked my childhood. My mother had gone into an eight year spiral of depression and psychiatric treatments six months after I was born. This was the result of attempting to witness to a neighbor who burned incense and kept her house dark. I had a real fear of Asians, and perhaps an inherently deeper fear of their foreign gods. After one visit with this Buddhist woman, I didn't have a mother for the next eight years. My mom had been raised in a loving Christian home, was very popular in school, adjusted well to marriage, and yet in this one encounter, instantly, her inner balance was gone.[13] Although she had now been delivered for a number of years, I was still wary of how an unprepared Christian can suddenly be ambushed. Good intentions don't compensate the person who loses this much time, and I had picked up a strong family aversion to anything that had a fortune cookie attached to it.

It is amazing how fears don't stay hidden. Until the decision of a trip to the Orient was looming in front of

---

[13] **see page 160**

me, I was not consciously aware that I was avoiding more than Chinese restaurants. I had been prayed over several times growing up and was told my feet would touch foreign soil many times. Like Jonah, I found out God will call you to your prejudices. So, of course, God places the Orient as His first choice on the itinerary. This *minor* detail of destination created a constant inner conflict in me about the entire trip. There is a little of Jonah in all of us which surfaces under pressure.

If I had wanted an external excuse not to go, people were providing one. Well-meaning friends began working on my parents to get them to intervene and keep me at home. Terrible stories of disaster were told and many attempts were made to insinuate my mom and dad were poor parents for even considering the idea of allowing me to go. I would walk up on intense conversations and hear every conceivable reason why this trip was not a good idea. The conscience issue was challenged—after all, smuggling Bibles into a communist country is a *criminal* offence (consequently, God could not give me any protection). This was played like the trump card. It was hard for my parents to answer their questions, their reasonings and predictions, and their horror stories of disaster with any real authority; one might say the circumstances of my going were a bit unusual. Others were sure that God had forbidden me to go and they were sent to warn us. Several even wanted the distinction of playing the rogue umpire who calls it before it happens. But one thing was sure, the general consensus was adamant: "She is too young to die!"

If there is any fear in a parent, it is played upon emotionally like the banging on the keys of an out-of-tune piano. A knot usually rises up in your stomach when you think you are a party to killing someone and my parents struggled with what to do with this knot! With all due respect and admiration to my parents who had raised me in a sheltered home, they gave me their blessing to go.

Within a few weeks of departure, we were still working out details and raising, in small amounts, money for Donna's trip. Friendly naysayers eventually brought to our attention, "You've waited too long. You no longer have time to get a passport back in the mail!" It had never occurred to us it takes a passport to go overseas! So my brother, Bill Ruth, Donna and I planned a trip to New Orleans—using the excuse of obtaining our passports to get in a couple of days at the World's Fair.

As we made the long drive to Louisiana, neither of us was completely positive we were going to China, and still reserved the right to back out—even if we had passports. On the way home, however, we saw a city limits sign that reported "China, Texas, population, 1351." Bill snapped our picture commemorating this random moment that hit us with the *seriousness* of an inside joke from above. Somehow, when we jumped back in the car, **we grasped that this was a confirmation sign that we were on our way!**

As the agent's hands in **San Francisco** moved rapidly across my anatomy in our first official frisk before boarding for Kaioshung, Taiwan, I made a joke to lighten up this sober woman. After 9-11, nothing of this nature could be said to a customs agent, but America was carefree and she was uptight and no one back home had informed me that in the U.S. it was legal to place hands where this lady was searching—so I dropped a verbal bomb to distract her.

Strangers around me let out a chorus groan, bemoaning their fate that I was on a smuggling team with them. Hoot-calls from hecklers punctuated and accentuated the lecture she gave me. Before we had even left American soil, I had already managed to make things much more complicated by having a sense of humor, only appreciated by small, select groups—namely, immediate family members and the people who gave birth to me. I think the customs lady gave me a more difficult time than usual and an extra thorough examination of my person, because of my mouth. No one had warned me that we had to mind our manners in the San Francisco airport.

Since, I had never been out of my Texas environment I learned an important life lesson: humor is localized. What we found comical wasn't necessarily amusing to the rest of the world; this Texan had made an appearance abroad for the first time. I jotted myself a mental note not to entertain anyone else in customs. The team made ongoing commentary about how they had found the weak link in the chain. This marked my first incident of *distinguishing* myself with my new friends.

We were persecuted for our race (being born *Southerners*), our youth, our small town thinking... and judged inferior on all accounts right from the start. Texans have a certain inborn worldview about themselves anyway, and I felt disjointed, like I was already among foreigners. I suspect I didn't do much to help change any stereotypical generalities among this very edgy group—over 200 people from all over North America who had banded together for crusades in the Far East, and more specifically, to smuggle Bibles into China. There was plenty of good-natured bantering, but only God can truly *unite a team* of strangers. The moment this happens in a mission team, no one has to explain it, you can sense it. We had *not* even left, and we could feel the lack of cohesiveness of the team and missed every reminder of home.

"Aisle seat please," I chirped, as I checked in. I hated heights, and the bulk of the trip through the Orient involved long flights. I would sit as far away from the window as possible and would never move until we landed. (I never ride roller coasters for similar reasons— I hate there being nothing but air between me and the ground.) It was a step of obedience to board the giant 747. Before I ever left home, I prayed preventatively God would deliver me from this fear and my mother had given me some very sound advice: *"Don't look out the window, just tell yourself you are on a Greyhound bus driving through road construction and you will do fine."*

Well, who knew how much I would need a mother's advice? During our journey we hit some exceptionally rough weather and it grew increasingly turbulent. Some of those who did not have the *Greyhound bus theory* were getting sick, picturing a plane bouncing in turmoil rather than a bus hitting a pothole.

One thing happened that distinguished the Christians from the other passengers. In all the years of traveling I have never seen this happen again—we hit an air pocket, and someone estimated that we dropped close to a thousand feet in seconds. This did not feel like a normal lurch, rather it felt like this massive plane was falling out of the sky. Passengers and stewardesses collapsed down in their seats screaming and covering their heads; but our team inadvertently threw their hands up in the air and shouted, "Hallelujah!" That makes quite an impact when there are 240 of us on the same plane who display the same reaction.

Of course, I was very peaceful, thinking about that terrible *pothole* and enjoying with amusement that, under pressure, Christians view *their time to go* with a lot more joy than someone who doesn't know where they are going. Since then, somewhere in unmarked time, high above the safety of ground, the Lord has delivered me from a fear of flying; I can look out of my plane windows and I no longer think about the bussing industry.

Bragging rights on any mission trip will be established on three major criteria: food, bathrooms, and custom inspections. When you hear missionaries get together, each person tries to top the other's story as *ranks of spirituality* are assigned with each level of difficulty.

Donna was a step ahead with her expertise in one field, already having gone on record as saying she is going to write a book mapping out the best and cleanest bathrooms in Texas because of her standing as the self proclaimed president of the IBBS.[14] The first thing I encountered in the Orient, on our connecting flight in Japan to Taiwan, was the shock of what they term a toilet. Donna did not have a category for this art form. They put porcelain over a hole in the floor. The *secret* was passed on and long lines of "Westerners" went to the bathroom, only to look and to photograph this oddity. This is the first picture in my scrapbook celebrating my first step in the Orient. Now, reflecting back to the places I have been through the years, I would consider that toilet the lap of luxury.[15]

I wasn't expecting such extravagant hotels overseas as the Kaohsiung Ambassador Hotel. Kaohsiung is a bustling city as technologically advanced as any Western metroplex, yet framed in a Chinese venue. With the

---

[14] Itty-Bitty Bladder Society.

[15] If some of the information is offensive to you, remember that my target group is youth. Realizing that parents might pick up a copy of this book, discretion has guided me in what I have shared and I have cut out a lot of humorous human interest stories in the attempt to relate to ALL readers. So if you would like to have known LESS, skip the paragraph and move on; if you yearn to know MORE, go with us on our next trip.

insatiable curiosity of an adventurer, I couldn't wait to explore the city, the open markets, the industrious people and the Love River gracing the front of our hotel. From my window I could just imagine what a stroll by that river would be like at night.

The smell *of the Love River* didn't quite live up to the images formed in my mind from its name. In fact there was much contrast in this city: on one side of the road—technology; on the other, raw meat hanging in the markets without any visible refrigeration. While most people shopped and rested, we explored. The people were very economical, zipping about with compact cars and motor scooters. I took pictures as proof that a family of five could ride on one scooter. Donna and I didn't waste a moment in our rooms or visiting with our team. After assisting with the crusade prayer teams late into the evenings, we would run out again into the bustling city at night to see how many people we could meet.

A Buddhist funeral passed by which I mistook for a parade rather than a funeral—with bouquets of cut flowers decorating each vehicle. Drawing near any of their shrines of worship, I felt a constricting band of pressure around my forehead—I had no interest in exploring any of their religious practices which were heavily entwined with their culture. It was overwhelming to me to think of so many Buddhists in one place.

Donna had a natural love for the people. (She talked incessantly about legally adopting children we visited in the orphanage in the mountains of Taiwan, and during her worst outbursts of emotion, I had to prevent her from kidnapping stranded Oriental children in crowds.) I, on the other hand, was perplexed at her tears and her fixation with the orphans. What a contrast in inclinations we were! I was puzzled at what was lacking in me. Several times I asked Donna to pray that in my heart I would fall in love with the Chinese people.

Prayer had its immediate physical hurdles; over-saturation kicked in the aftermath of our first crusade—people pressed against people created a claustrophobic sensation in the summer heat. There were so many people to try to get used to all at once and I felt compressed, like I was a trapped sardine drowning in soy sauce. Even in the ladies room I couldn't find solace. This bathroom was a gigantic room for all to share, with no stalls, no toilets—just a concrete floor. The custodians came in every hour and used hoses to spray it off. [16] The smell was terribly rank. I faced a week's itinerary of being packed together into those stifling meetings and I was sure that having air conditioning in the building could have at least aided Donna's prayers for my soul.

The revival services would end with an altar call and the stadium would unload until every person possible was at the altar. One might picture orderly "*lines*"in prayer-lines, but each of us was smothered into the mass hysteria similar to groupies mobbing a rock star. It felt like death by suffocation awaiting us at the front each night. A virtual

---

[16] No picture taken. I took my camera in, but couldn't bring myself to take the picture. There are some moments you do not want to capture!

sea of Oriental bodies clinging to us—a mass of slimy, wet humanity drenched from the heat. The first night of the crusade I went back to my hotel in shock—much like an army recruit who realized he had been promised something different and had already signed a long contract.

I prayed in quiet desperation, *"Lord, please put a love for these people in my heart."* I was overdosing on the Orient and it was our first stop of several before we were in mainland China.

On the second night of the crusade, I saw two fresh, eager faces of teenage-looking girls sitting in the bleachers of this indoor stadium. The Lord impressed upon me, "I want you to go up there to talk to them." I counter-prayed, "Lord, no, no... You make it clear if it is really You." I went up to the rail and out of thousands of people, our eyes locked. They smiled and worked their way out of the throng, then came running down the final steps toward me. The two girls just fell into my arms. Pressing against me in a tight abandoned hug, it dawned on me they were both pregnant. It was a chance awkward meeting between strangers, but we made an immediate connection. Somehow, at the same time I had picked them, they had picked me. Overseas for the first time, I had seen the masses, but now I was seeing the individuals.

The girls (it is impossible to tell age in this country because of great complexions) indicated by a form of charades that they wanted me to pray for their unborn babies. I was touched with the girl's humility—desiring me to pray and bless them. And then it happened:

The Lord just baptized me in His love for the Chinese people.[17] Their only communication was tears when I prayed; none of us understood one word the other had said. Ministry broke the barrier of my past. At that moment it happened. In an instant, I realized I was no longer seeing them as Orientals, but as people.

No sooner had I finished praying, another person was vying for my attention. A *non-stop crying woman* is nerve-wracking as it is, but especially impossible if you don't understand the language—even if she had stopped the hysteria long enough to explain herself. In desperation, an American had brought her to me: she was crying a soul-wrenching wail like I've never heard in a human cry. I felt a tenderness for her and prayed for everything that came to mind, but obviously it wasn't helping. After half an hour of agonizing, soul-wrenching, pitiful cries, as I stood helplessly with her head buried on my shoulder, I determined, "I can't stand this one more minute. I hate this language barrier; I have to find out what is tormenting this lady." There were about three people on our team who could interpret Chinese and I was determined to find one of them. I searched through the whole, people-locked mob and found one of the guys at the far end of the stadium stage.

As we worked our way through the crowd, I told him his mission, "Please tell us why this woman is crying uncontrollably." I was born with an insatiable

---

[17] If you go to the mission field and don't have a love for the people, I am a breathing example that the Lord can fix you and supernaturally give you the love.

case of curiosity, but what I was about to hear almost cured it. I was in shock as the English words fell on my ears, and I tried to absorb what I was hearing. Three months before she had lost her baby when she had somehow boiled it, and it died. The translator repeated over and over, "in hot water!" as if I would understand. *Don't ask me "Why?" or "Was it an accident?"* I don't know myself. I asked direct, probing questions which were translated to her, but the only answers I received were horrible, agonizing, pitiful human cries. There are some things in life you have to make peace with because you will never know.

Despite the fact that we had no comprehension of what their needs were—these people had deep needs and they were usually ten times worse than anything we could fathom. After that, we were never again compelled to ask, "What are we praying for?" We just prayed.

Like déjà vu, Taiwan reconstructed a scene from my past where, previously I had not prevailed. God not only had broken down the walls of my prejudices and cynical mentality, but He had reenacted those childhood emotional camps of tears and hugging, *sans[18] someone strumming the guitar, singing the fourth round of Kum-ba-ya.* Suddenly, I wasn't the critic, neither was I aloof and I pressed right back into the people. It is my experience that God keeps re-issuing a test until we pass.

---

[18] Half my American proof-readers assumed this word meant "with" which is the exact opposite concept. *Sans* is French for "without".

It is time to swap tales about the food: on this first mission field we had octopus... we had chicken with its claws still on the toes. Taiwanese chew on a claw the way we chew on a drumstick. We had fish with their *heads on* and their *eyes bulging* and their *teeth still grimacing*.

A group of appreciative pastors, wanting to thank us for sharing a few words of encouragement at their churches, *overpaid* us by taking us to eat in a fancy restaurant. Large black toads were frantically swimming in a glass jar on display as we entered the door of this well-to-do eatery. Donna looked nervous.

I asked the cashier, "Do these toads make people hungry? What are these toads advertising for you? Are they decoration or food? "

She told me enthusiastically, "You choose your toad you would like to eat, and we prepare it the way you like!" I guess we were dining at the Taiwanese version of Red Lobster—choosing your own dinner out of the water. The main difference was the appearance of warts on these black toads and the color of the aquarium. I was mesmerized by the continual motion of their legs. Donna realized I was missing and came back to tear me away from watching these toads do their aerobics so I could be seated with the rest of the group (not for my sake, but hers). Donna looked at the platter of fish displayed by the waiter. She did not appreciate the fish on plate looking back at her and smiling. I realized then all my practice *eating at a Chinese restaurant back home* two weeks before departure was a failed project.

Donna switched places until I was in the chair next to her before we placed our order. I had seriously meditated on that verse, *"Eat what is set before you,"* but I was increasingly troubled that Donna's near hyperventilation was going to be *a poor witness* of American appreciation for the hospitality of these people. But what the waiter served next was to be the ultimate test of her character. He placed a chicken in front of her with claws, head, beak and eyes. I mused for a moment Donna was going to faint. She stated tartly: "I can't eat anything that is staring at me!" So I put my napkin over its eyes. Again she complained, "Please cut my piece of chicken—I can't look at its face anymore."

Uncovering the shrouded body, I obliged and sawed off her first bite. Guilt attacks would stab me periodically through the course of the lunch over our raucous manners. It became obvious that covering over Donna's behavior was hopeless. I have no idea if we failed or passed the admonition of that Scripture...

One could starve in the midst of an abundance of food with those chopsticks, but maybe it is for the best in foreign countries. However, the pastors had a plan to take care of any starvation we might be experiencing from being issued chopsticks—when we finished one course, they would call for more menus and order another course.

I, naturally, asked the pastors to draw pictures of what Donna was eating to help her with the menu language-barrier and for the sheer sake of the entertainment value she provided. In my scrapbook I still have the napkin with the doodles of the octopus, black eggs and other fine delicacies. The men seemed determined to let us try everything Taiwan had to offer.

I guess our outrageous behavior was considered charming rather than offensive to these gracious pastors because these men insisted on giving us their neckties that stated in Chinese: *God Loves the World's People*, which we proudly wore as a sash over our Sunday dresses on the way back to our hotel.

We looked forward with eager anticipation to what was in store for us on the remainder of this trip. There is something about being immersed in another culture that will bring out the best and the worst in a person and Taiwan had equally challenged us individually. We had joined this tour with private reservations and hang-ups. Donna and I had, each in our own way, made our peace with our first exposure to the Orient.

Usually I measure a trip *daily* by the standard— "the whole trip was worthwhile for just this *one thing* that happened..." and although so much more was shortly destined to occur, the experiences in Taiwan settled some important issues. It was the foundation of God's tutoring.

Taiwan, which had started out as such a culture shock to my system, in five short days felt like home away from home. God had settled something in me with the first country. Nationality was now celebrated and my old fears were instantly gone. The Christians in other places no longer felt like foreigners, but like family I was meeting for the *first* time.

CHAPTER THREE
Beauty and Poverty

BEACHES! PALM TREES! WAVES! I thought we were exploring future possibilities for a honeymoon site rather than *suffering* on a mission field. Donna threw open the balcony door to breathe in the ocean air. We were on a whirlwind tour out of Taiwan and onto the Philippines where, in three days, I would fall utterly in love at first sight with the people and beauty of this country.

Not even ominous warnings about the danger of this place could spoil its beauty. The team briefing before our evening banquet meal sternly warned us to watch for pickpockets—even within our beautiful Philippine Plaza Hotel. Instructions for that night stated that Manila was the worst place to travel because unemployment was so high and the crime rate was alarming. Our orders were: "Keep your doors locked, your belongings in safe keeping and, in general, be *on the alert.*" This advice was delivered in the same tone my mother used when she wanted to make an impression. We listened *attentively.*

Donna and I raced up to our room to unpack. With this kind of splendor it was hard to imagine any kind of trouble. Out our bay window the ships, sun and seagulls gave us an ever-changing panorama of sky touching water. We settled in quite comfortably. That first night

I was sleeping peacefully when Donna came over, roughly shook my bed and ordered me, "Get up! Get up!" I asked, "What's wrong?" Her face looked serious as she explained, "I'm scared and we need to read Psalm 91; I just don't feel at peace and we need protection." We could sense something was wrong but we didn't know what. The minute she finished reading Psalm 91 out loud to me, I fell back to sleep and Donna continued to pray.

The next morning after a thorough search, we couldn't find our room key. Whoever was knocking on our door seemed indignant, just by the forceful manner in which he pounded. We opened it to a smartly dressed hotel employee holding our key, "Ladies, you slept with the key in your door all night long." He said it with the poise of a butler but the tone of a parent. Our skills at navigating the foreign fields amazed me.

What was more disheartening than our own incompetence was the management freely using their own keys to enter our room at any given time. These internationals had developed their own rules of etiquette. My mom had one request: I must wear a money belt like a dog wears his collar. (Mother's utter terror was that I would lose my passport while I was abroad, so this was her final concession. I was not allowed to remove it for any reason, day or night.) Obedient kid that I was—hygiene aside, I showered in my money belt[19] with the passport safely tucked in the zippered pocket. While I was in the shower, the "*kind*" young bellboy used his own key to enter, bringing me a vase of fresh cut flowers. He nonchalantly attempted to present me this *extra* hotel amenity. I was trapped! Donna had skipped out to lunch to begin her usual networking, so I started yelling for this young man, whose face I'm looking at—to back out of the bathroom. He started rapidly explaining to me in his native language, *Tagalog*, he didn't understand English. I spoke to him in a universal language I was sure he understood—LOUD! (It was apparent that in a foreign country it made little difference if we left our key in the door since they felt free to use their own.)

After lunch we were given choices from a long list of ministry sites. Donna and I both settled on the leper colony. Up until that time, I didn't know that leprosy still existed in the world, assuming that it was only a disease of Biblical times. Our interest was sparked by the brochure they eagerly handed us that had typed in English: *The Tala Leprosarium is the home for 2,053 patients and a community of 20,000 souls of former lepers and their dependents.* The colony was almost identical in size to our hometown of Brownwood, and it was hard for me to imagine a parallel population consisting of lepers and

---

[19] My dutiful compliance left a three week imprinted ring around my waist. I ceremoniously removed the belt upon my return home to Texas soil and that is why this book has nothing appealing to relate in the way of good stories of lost passport incidents.

immediate families. They have their own type of government, their own little store—their own little everything. I guess no one wants to include them in the general population.

Norma Tinio was our ministry host. She wore a bright red, silk dress and black, high heel pumps, and it amazed me how she moved toward us like a lightning bolt. It was obvious she had made up her mind about the two of us when she pushed us toward the bus, "Now look, you two are going with me—first class with air conditioning."[20] Proud of what she had to offer, she loaded us on a large bus and grasped the microphone in her hands. I kicked back to listen to local historical facts on our tour. She told our group her father was a general in the Filipino army which formally ended her sharing anymore background information. The woman started preaching a full sermon with all the frills and extras—which lasted throughout the hour and a half drive.

I commented to Donna, "I'm glad we have a seat near the front; this is better than any revival sermon   I have ever heard." Norma walked up and down the aisle of the bus loudly praying for our members, some who were very receptive and some who were wide-eyed with surprise. I have always been amazed at the fiery, passionate preachers the Filipino people produce. (When I arrived at the leper colony I found out why it was such a good sermon—she was trying to get our fickle American

---

20 Other teams had less favorable, localized transportation.

faith level built up.) She had preached from the beginning of that tour to the end.

I don't know *what* I was expecting, but leprosy was *more wretched, more horrifying than one can imagine.* But the lepers didn't seem to be aware of our fear; they were lined up, hands reaching out, each wanting to be touched. I surmised that they had not received much physical contact in their lives, and they wanted to make up for lost time. I had not made up my mind whether I wanted to touch a leper, so this *reception line* was quite a shock to me. I resisted the urge to look for any open sores on my body. Their sores were violent looking and I cringed at the thought of making contact. However, the lepers made up my mind for me and they embraced me as if I were a long, lost relative.

I had a new appreciation for Jesus' ministry among the lepers and found relief in the fact that when He laid hands on the sick—*they got better and He never got sick!* I called to Him in a quick prayer under my breath, "Be big within me." I had some personal beliefs on healing as a doctrinal issue, but this is where theory collides with reality—when a person who has an obviously contagious disease with oozing wounds wants to hug you. Therefore, the *"do I touch or do I not?"* decision was made for us right off the bus, not based on scriptural assurance, but by the fact that they were *quick!*

They called it a hospital, but it looked more like an army barrack from the previous century. Donna took one look at me and whispered, "Check out that lizard over cot number two!" The only fact that conveyed to us this was a hospital was girls wearing white dresses with starched caps, rolling little carts of IVs.

Terminal cases on the floor, rather than in beds, army buildings, modern nurses, and roaming lizards made us repeatedly do double takes trying to absorb what we were seeing. The eclectic combination played upon our minds when we tried to fit it all into the definition of a *serious* hospital.

Norma stood out in the middle and we stood huddled in a tight circle, clinging to each other. All too soon, she prayed and dispersed us with a cheery— "Okay, now go lay hands on the lepers."

I felt frozen, deep in thought: Leprosy had felt so safe as a *Biblical* term. I believed Jesus healed the sick ever since my Baptist Sunday School teacher had taught me those stories with felt-board displays. However, reality never seemed so prevalent, as history managed to zoom to the present in such glaring, unfriendly terms. I don't know if I would have ever moved from that spot, but I think God showed me something at that moment to build my confidence. My eyes fell on one woman who was sitting on a cot, gently ministering to these horrible-beyond-belief cases lying on pallets, stretched out on the concrete. She had taken her children with her and they were following her example. The children were beautiful and near our age, one was seventeen and the other twenty-two. Any mother who would take her children into a leper colony—*knew that she knew that she knew* that God would not call her anywhere that He would not protect her. Healing and protection were the two issues on the Biblical lab table. And the class was no longer *theory*, but was now in session! It was time I had to make a move.

Most of our team compassionately gravitated to the most pathetic cases—heart-wrenching, pitiful situations beyond any human condition we had imagined from Biblical narratives. The room had a hierarchy arrangement of survivor-based assumptions. The lepers on the beds were pathetic, but appeared to have more of a chance to live, while the lepers lying on the floor were in the obvious last stages. The very sight turned my stomach. Noses and eyes were eaten away by the disease and hands and feet were ravaged by this plague—masses of human bodies marred in ways I never conceived possible. Unintentionally, I would find myself turning my head to wince in private horror. The guide explained that in this wing of the hospital, the skin of these people would be charcoal-colored with texture like leather.[21] Reports were circulating that since Norma had been ministering to

---

[21] They had explained to us that there were three types of leprosy – the first kind had skin like ash that flaked off in layers and had the texture of black leather. The second had very hard bumps, which were tender and terrible looking. Some of their bodies had giant bumps all over the surface. The third were patients with open wounds – raw sores that continuously oozed infection. All three types were in this hospital. Some of them just had one type and others had combinations of it.

them, their skin had become pliable and another testimony claimed that a couple of lepers who had been committed for life were out in one week. In the past, people would go there to live and die, but now the hospital was having a turnover. Through this woman's ministry of fervent prayer and God's Word—people were *leaving* rather than *dying*.

I avoided the gross cases and kept searching before I knelt to pray with a frail thirteen-year-old boy. I purposely looked around for anyone who would not turn my stomach—who had nothing missing, nothing oozing.

"Where are you from?" Uncomfortable with initial encounters, I asked this boy an irrelevant, leading question. I picked him out because he lacked any obvious signs of the disease. His voice was barely audible as he answered, "My parents are lepers."

Mechanically, I tried to switch gears into a conversation involving spiritual matters. It felt awkward, attempting to make an inroad between this sullen boy and myself, but I forced myself to press through. I hate to admit it, but I was young in my faith and it worried me to think about sitting on the bed of someone who had leprosy. In moments like that, your focal point is either on *yourself*, on the *other person*, or upon *the power of God*. (I've since discovered that shyness and bashfulness, which pretend to be such humble servants, are actually a form of self-focus.) Thankfully, a lady from our team joined me, took over ministering to the boy, and the Lord moved on him. I had vacillated with my heart, focused incorrectly and was as unsteady as a wave on the sea, tossed by the wind. However, God's classrooms of instruction can move rapidly, and in retrospect, it is amazing the difference between what I learned from that room to the next...

I looked over at Norma and admired her courage to take a very practical faith to her people. She was a striking example to me of what true ministry looks like. After Bible school, most people search for a more comfortable assignment with a desk, a window and a permanent salary, but not Norma.

It struck me that the women in the Philippines are paradoxes. This next episode emphasized in high contrast the extremely outgoing personalities of some of the women once they converted, against the introverted personalities of the culture—as you will see next.

The distressed nurses burst through the hospital doors as if they were cattle on a roundup, driven by an unseen force. Suddenly, Norma appeared through the doors right behind them, chasing them like a bolt of lightning. Always in a state of perpetual action, Norma maneuvered the group to the women's ward. All the while she was in the process of evangelizing the nurses, despite the fact they had flatly refused her appeal.

When Norma popped the question, "Would you like to be saved?" the timid nurses responded with a definite, "No!" Not to be deterred, Norma was herding them down the hospital aisle and they were running from her. I was just watching, really watching, and dumbfounded at the boldness of this woman. I couldn't help marveling at her, "I've never seen this style of evangelism!"

It startled me out of my deep-in-thought scrutiny of her methods when Norma suddenly called out my name, "Angie, pray for the women in this sickbay!" True to form, she instructed me to voice the prayer out loud for the whole group. With a force much like the pull of gravity, Norma had drawn another reluctant one into her circle.

Not aided by any special spiritual emotions, I was overwhelmed at the sight of the lepers, the hopeless look of the situation and the sickening smell, but I did as I was told. I didn't feel any particular power; I just lifted one hand and called on God for help. I remember I felt the prayer from the bottom of my heart. No sooner had I finished, (I'm not even sure I had the *"...in Jesus Christ's Name, Amen,"* out) when one of the oldest lepers hastily rose up and made her way toward us. In my heart I was praying specifically for leprosy, so what God did next surprised me.

This weather-beaten, old woman was pointing at her ears and shouting something in her native tongue until one of the group translated in the excitement. She was motioning at her ears, crying in Tagalog, "I've been healed! I've been healed! I can hear! I can hear!"

Norma didn't even take a second look at the ecstatic woman; she turned to those nurses and asked, "Is it true?

Was this woman deaf?" As if to answer, they began to snap their fingers near her ears as the sobbing, old woman nodded emphatically she could hear the snaps. The reserved little nurses then broke down and started crying, saying, "Yes, yes. She was completely deaf." Like a true evangelist who sees God's hand in miracles to be a sign to unbelievers, Norma seized the impact of the situation and trumpeted, "*Now* are you ready to accept the Lord?" It was a completely different scene from minutes before; they were very willing and ready converts. I stood there, never moving, never praying with another individual in those barracks, just staring at what I was witnessing—three hungry, petite nurses huddled in a circle, earnestly praying the sinner's prayer... with Norma.

~

The next day we chose a second ministry site among Manila's poorest of poor and our new hosts loaded us into a custom decorated jeepney—a painted tin can interpretation of a jeep, with swinging apparatus clanking around—like the interior of a peddler's wagon. A jeepney's size is comparable to an enclosed pickup truck, which can hold ten to twelve passengers, if I recall correctly. The driver told us without cracking a smile, "Americans have to pay *double* because they take up *twice* as much room!" I looked and we did; and he charged us and we paid!

Donna and I had chosen the squatter's village – reported to be the very poorest of the poor.[22] Hanging

---

[22] See pages 21-23 for a further discussion of the story.

clothes were flapping in the breeze, making it look like a city of flags. Carefully planning our steps, we were walking in open sandals through exposed sewage. These houses looked like something a child would build. It was amazing how many family members could be packed into these makeshift homes of cardboard and tin.

The ministry hosts seated us outside and instructed, "We want you to give them your testimonies." Out of all the times of my life, this was one of the most humbling experiences—sitting there wondering what I could possibly say that could do any good for their lives. The crowd grew from fifteen people to about forty in seconds. We were tightly pressed together as the crowd swelled. There was a noticeable distinction among the people—some of them had sparkles in their eyes, but most had very dull, empty eyes that had long before given up hope.

Using an interpreter when my turn came, I shared with them about my family. "At one point my family was almost wrecked. My mom was sick and many feared she would be institutionalized. My dad turned to the Lord and vowed, 'If Christianity is real, I want You to do something to help us; and if there is not anything to Christianity, then I want out!'" I told these words of my father with the same fury as if they were my own. Then, I directed it back to my audience, "God can take this brokenness and He can restore any life given to Him. This is the whole reason why Donna and I are here—because we are a testimony that He can fix broken lives."

I cheated, took a shortcut and used my parent's testimony, but immediately I internally vowed never to do that again. Something fought in me to have my own testimony and I almost felt angry at heaven for using a *borrowed* one. (*Little did I know that one week from this moment I would forever have my own!*) A call to respond was given after I spoke and about fifteen people came up and received the Lord. There were young boys, teenagers, and old women and men at the altar.[23]

Afterwards, they brought us to the ministry host's home to celebrate our visit, and it was there, at that moment, I fell in love with the humility and generosity of the Filipino family. I had an urge to feed these people, but instead, they shared what they had with us. These folks looked so poor that it was all I could do to eat their food in front of them. For the duration of our visit, the family sat without the aid of chairs, as a catcher would squat at a baseball game. They placed us in their chairs. Sympathetically, my legs hurt just looking at each of them hunkered down, chair-less. This custom looked so primitive. I had this regal picture in my mind of Father Abraham from scriptures, of how he stood so straight and tall, but now I wondered if he looked more like this small, wrinkled, eighty-*ish* year old man on his haunches in the corner like a tent dweller. Perhaps the dignified Bible characters looked a lot like these humble people.

---

[23] I recommend that *new* missionaries go to the Philippines for their first overseas mission trip; Filipinos are unusually responsive to evangelism.

The hospitality trays, laden with Coca-Colas™ and candy snacks, that these people served our team made us feel uncomfortable. Their modest lives combined with radical generosity were a bit overwhelming. Being Americans, we tried to decline because it is humbling, almost revolting, for someone to give us something out of their poverty; but they had a way (or more of a cultural art form) of convincing us not to refuse. The family's cheerfulness and kindheartedness stayed in my mind after I turned in for bed that night. **There is nothing like a third world country to demonstrate your life contrasted against the widow's mite.**[24]

~

This trip was a time for examining and reflecting on my own upbringing, and I felt like an outsider even among my own peers. I was constantly asked, *"What did you say? Could you say that again?"* My Texas accent was a novelty to this "American" hodgepodge group and was a constant source of teasing. What they didn't know is that even my fellow Texans often had a difficult time with the way I could butcher the language. I had never thought much about this, but suddenly my tongue felt very thick and I was often asked to repeat myself. Some things one never forgets. The team leaders appeared to get great pleasure out of asking me questions about growing up and about life in a small town. One queried as to how much

---

[24] Luke 21: 2-3

stock my dad had and I answered back, "About 53 head on 157 acres." The shock froze on his face.

Donna often acted as my interpreter, deciphering Texas idioms into Californian lingo, but even *she* couldn't figure out what had happened in the translation on that one. She and I discussed it, and everyone exploded in laughter at the difference of our two worlds when we reworked his question. I was thinking Angus and Hereford, and they were thinking Merrill Lynch and municipal bonds. Anytime I was introduced on the trip, this story was repeated with the introduction. I felt like I had been raised in a hole, but I never seriously minded their good-natured jabs. Teasing can often be a backhanded compliment, and this opened up some honest relationships. Despite our diversities, many in-depth talks about a personal walk with the Lord went on in private moments that not even colloquial differences could hinder.

It was as if life could change in a moment just by rounding invisible corners. We had sacred moments and we had light-hearted banter; a carefree moment could quickly change into hair-raising narrow escapes.

Embedded in my mind is an unforgettable scene from one of the nightly Philippine crusades that hosted thousands of people. A gigantic crystal chandelier fell in the middle of the worship service in an auditorium jam packed with Filipino people. Nearer than I would like to have been, I happened to be directly facing this gigantic light fixture when it tore loose from the ceiling and fell into a room packed to capacity. Appearing to drop in slow motion, I braced myself for the impact. It crashed, shattering crystal and spraying glass in every direction. I would hate to try to guess the size of that chandelier, but it had an enormous frame—the largest I had ever seen, suspended high in a cathedral-type ceiling. It fell directly into a spacious aisle landing like a perfect fit of the last piece of a puzzle. Seeing it drop into a crowded crusade with no one hurt defied all human rationalization. The massive size could have injured more than a dozen just in its diameter alone. Only on the other side of heaven will we finally know the full accounts of all the things from which God has spared us. The revival hosts paused, prayed, and then continued.

We squeezed in all the adventures we possibly could during those three days in the Philippines. I could not get enough. When I stepped up to board the plane, I wheeled around facing outside one last time and declared, as General MacArthur once decreed, "I shall return!" Donna looked at me in shock because I have no flair for drama. But even I didn't realize how quickly God had planned for my return.

~

Many times the Asian people will "convert" just to be polite and not hurt a person's feelings. They see it as good manners to tell a person what they want to hear. However, if it is an authentic conversion another problem arises. They must prepare for a family assault on their newfound faith; otherwise, they will melt back into their Buddhist homes and ancestral worship[25] and totally forget the claims of Christ. It is a difficult mission field in many ways.

In Tokyo,[26] we met the teenage brother of an international student we had befriended in Brownwood. After many failed attempts at pronouncing his long Japanese name, we aborted the effort and christened him Taco. The difficult enunciation fit well with this abbreviation, and he became quite attached to his new tag.

We invited him into our hotel room in an attempt to get him away from his peers so we could share the gospel without distractions. As he followed us to our room, he looked in every direction, walked tightly against the wall, hid behind doors at every opportunity and looked both ways before entering our room. We were rather alarmed because we had no idea what was affecting his behavior. Considering how we saw ourselves as *so much older and more mature in our early twenties*, it never crossed our minds that we had committed a cultural impropriety.

Donna didn't lose any time doing a very thorough job of presenting the Gospel and he looked very attentive, *until* she came to the verse "For all have

---

[25] or whatever the case may be

[26] Author's note: At this point, I have inserted an event out of the chronological order of our itinerary for the sake of the flow of the overall story and climax of smuggling.

sinned..." He abruptly stopped her and interrupted with, "I've never sinned."

Donna tried to help Taco *remember* some of his sins but he persisted – *"I have never sinned!"* I was quite amused at her helpful list for him to choose from. Knocked off balance, she looked at me and bluntly avowed, "I don't know what to do now," and just quit. I think she wanted me to suggest some sin she hadn't thought of as a possibility.

I chided her, "Keep going with the verses— the Holy Spirit has helped you so far!" She protested, "I can't! That was a memorized presentation, and the person *must admit* he is a sinner before we can proceed to the next point!"

I laughed; my impressive partner had bailed. In America we never had anyone claim they had never sinned, and I had to admit it did create quite an impasse. After praying for a few minutes, I felt impressed that he had a huge emptiness in his life—often at night, he would cry out over the void. He agreed, "Yes! Yes! That is true. I am very empty and it is worse at night." He eagerly prayed with us.

I asked forgiveness for what I was about to do, then we confiscated Gideon Bibles in unlocked hotel rooms written in both Japanese and English. With much pomp and ceremony, we presented them as a gift from the American people to the Japanese converts during our stay and signed their names with ours in the *stolen* Bibles. When we returned stateside, out of twinges of conscience, we made extra contributions to the Gideon Association at the annual meeting for robbing Bibles on location.

Our team stayed nowhere long. Tokyo was just a two-day sampler on the tray of the Orient. I loved meeting new people and as much as we traveled, it offered many opportunities. Our departure flight was particularly memorable as I met people among our team members whom I had only read about. One pair I met worked for the Brother Andrew Open Doors Association. They were Bible couriers into Russia and what tales of adventure they told! Meeting them offered me a huge advantage over reading; now I could ask endless questions. I pumped them for all kinds of information. On these planes I could never sleep, so I used this time to learn from anyone who was awake.

CHAPTER FOUR

Twas the Night Before!

O H, ENCHANTING HONG KONG! I lifted my camera as I stepped onto the de-boarding ramp of our plane and snapped a picture of my first view of the city against the mountains. Instantly, a guard snatched the camera from my hands, exclaiming in heavily accented English, "You have taken a picture of *forbidden* area!" His hands tried to force open the back of my camera. I reached over and rescued my camera from his prying fingers. He was flabbergasted at my interception and continued to try to confiscate the roll. I used the film spool to feign a jammed camera, demonstrating an unsnapped picture. He was un-sympathetic, but his reason for the seizure was now denied. Inadvertently, I had dramatized a faulty camera with one horror on my mind—the last pictures on the roll were the most gorgeous Philippine sunsets over the bay.[27]

---

[27] This is the correct chronological order of the trip: Taiwan, Philippines, Hong Kong, China, and Tokyo. However, for the sake of the flow of the trip and to end with the highlight of smuggling, I interjected Tokyo into the main body of the trip.

Hong Kong was more guarded and mysterious than I had expected. Who knows what I accidentally had taken a picture of that made him think he had the right to remove my film. I have studied the picture and have seen nothing of interest that could get him so riled—perhaps I should sell it on eBay.

From the peak of the unloading ramp of the plane, the panorama begged to be photographed, but I had to resist—at least until I was out of reach from this very first man I met in Hong Kong. I gasped at the bay scene. Primitive Chinese junk boats were crisscrossing paths with ocean-liners. Never-ending skyscrapers struck me as a peculiar backdrop for this spectacular view of heavy water traffic on the inlet. All the motion mixed with the timeless serene landscape is compelling to the soul. Hong Kong has been correctly alluded to as the *Pearl of the Orient.*

I had understood British Hong Kong was very Westernized in its thought and culture, but I experienced a much more rigid society than I had anticipated. Apparently, the officials had the mind-set there were *unmarked* forbidden camera shots for Westerners. When I noticed tanks laden with soldiers rolling down the main street in broad daylight, I ran to our street corner to get a better camera angle and watched to see if any more "Chinese guards" would appear. We were in a British-ruled Hong Kong and I was shocked at how militaristic it had become even before it was formally returned to China.

Hong Kong was like a city that couldn't make up its mind. It was British, but it was Chinese. It was

Western, and it was Far Eastern. It was free enterprise, yet it gave the feeling Big Brother was watching. Tanks rolling down the street—that's not something you see in Texas on an ordinary day. It is definitely the *land between*. It was just that I didn't know **between WHAT** at the time! I had never seen communism in action!

Hong Kong shopping, however, was everything we expected it to be. The stores were beckoning us early in the morning. Donna and I dashed for the international trade buildings that could turn anyone into a compulsive buyer. Hong Kong has such an international flair; people from all corners of the world create a world market and a shopper's paradise. We navigated to the larger buildings with floors of shops. We steeled ourselves against the noticeable stares of men in ancient garb. Their eyes bored a hole in us with the unblinking stare of a reptile. Donna was purposely avoiding any prolonged contact with these men, so she let several available elevators pass without us.

Donna commandeered us into the first available elevator with a lone woman clothed in traditional dress. "What does that dot on your forehead *mean*?" Donna asked, assuming the whole world spoke English.

A random incident took place in that elevator which did not fit the usual interchange between inquisitive Americans and mysterious Middle Easterners. The lady removed the dot from her forehead and like a hammer on a nail, positioned it between Donna's eyes and exited on the next floor without saying a word.

I could not keep from dissolving into laughter at the look on Donna's face. Then to keep the drama going, I cautioned her with utmost authority, "Those dots are their wedding rings. She is tired of her husband and you just inherited him! When we hit ground level, he will be waiting for you!" Of course, I was making up my own fill-in-facts and Donna was so taken aback by the lady's nonverbal response that she promptly removed the dot in case there was any truth to what I said.

It was my turn to experience the unexpected as we headed to the hotel with bags of souvenirs for our friends back home. I heard a shot and saw a man fall on the sidewalk. A crowd quickly gathered around him and, of course, I moved in to get a closer look. Donna was not interested in my investigation. I guess she assumed there could be *more* gunfire from wherever that had come, so she grabbed my arm from that circle of gawkers and told me to "Run!"

She took off. I took off behind her, more for the reason of not losing her in that no-value-for-personal-space crowd than for calling an end to my investigative work. I saw her moving quickly away, back in the direction of the hotel; and without glancing around in my direction, she continued snapping me orders to follow her—*now!* Crossing a road was not foremost on my mind; I was looking back, interested in that crowd gathered around the wounded man. The driver of a nearby taxi was *also* looking at the crowd around the man. His brakes screeched to a halt, but it was too late. The next thing I knew, I was struck by the taxi and I was flying through the air. I landed on his hood with my face staring at his, with only his windshield separating us. I burst into laughter when I looked at his shocked face so close to mine. He laughed when he saw my response. It was one of those rare moments of human connection between strangers—a *chance meeting* between taxi cab driver and American pedestrian.

Donna never noticed. If God had not intervened I could have lain on that pavement like the man shot on the sidewalk. I was trying to yell for her to stop, but she was still moving at an increasing rate of speed. She didn't think bullets and shopping mixed.

At the crosswalk to the hotel front, I grabbed Donna by the arm and said with no extra emotion, "Since I've last seen you, I've been hit by a taxi!" She studied my face with a long stare trying to detect some hint of jest in my earnest eyes. Donna, who played *the mother hen role* at times, mumbled something incoherent about what could happen to me in five seconds out of her sight. "It is my way of meeting new people," I said, as if to answer her implausible shock I could find trouble that fast.

This was some place for a country girl to see how the other half lives and I was determined to see it all. Donna and I, with our party, took a ferry over to the Peak Tower Restaurant, whose view of the city at night took our breath away—but we lost only one breath... for Donna was sure we could take in all of Hong Kong in one night.

As I peered into the window of a dress shop, I saw people I recognized from the team. Inquisitively, Donna and I entered as the tailor noted on a pad his quick measurements of the customers. I envied the familiarity these veterans (members of our team who had taken this tour before) had with this city. They were choosing the most amazing fabrics to have custom-made suits ready upon their return from China. They matter-of-factly informed the tailor they would pick up their order in three days after returning from what would be the most daring aspect of our trip. I took their optimism of three days as *a sign* we would be back without any unexpected delays or detainments.

That night, at our team banquet, we got the *China prep and pep* talk. It detailed an elementary overview of communism, its stance against Christianity and its hatred of the Bible. We were given instructions on what we could and could not say until we left the People's Republic of China. The Bibles were no longer referred to except by the code name *bread* and we no longer referred to ourselves as a traveling crusade team. We were now officially tourists and had to remove all ID from our luggage that associated us with any ministry organizations. Our mission coordinators asked us to avoid personal witnessing for the sake of the secrecy of the Bibles. We were to avoid direct questions about God. They cautioned us that periodically the people who picked us up the next morning to take us to the train station would be *implanted government* spies to determine *the mission* of the group. "Remember, you are being watched and listened to at all times!" they warned. Even our wallets and purses had to be emptied of anything that linked us to Christian organizations. If they asked about God, we had to ignore their questions and concentrate on the work that the underground church would do to reach the people with our Bibles. They informed us the train would have people planted to listen to our conversations. Upon entering the country, official customs agents would search our luggage and there was no way to predict what would happen at that point. Hopefully, most of the Bibles would make it safely through, and if we managed to get them across the border, they warned us our rooms in China would be bugged and often searched when we left to *tour*. They read a verse from Scripture, dismissed the team, and told us, "Good night and sleep well!"

The Chinese Bibles were piled in heaps on the tables in the back of the room for us to pick up on our way out. I was fascinated by these paperback books which were written from right to left in a language that looked like a secret code. There was quite a bit of groaning at the foyer tables; each of us had an allotted ten to pack into our luggage before morning. Many around me were bemoaning having to carry something as cumbersome as books back to their rooms, as if it were the most difficult task they had to face on this trip.

An ironic sequence of events began to transpire. As we were deliberating over secrets and strategies as to how to carry them across in our bag, Donna and I were blessed with even more Bibles when other people decided that ten were too many and lightened their load to one or two. Several people put their Bibles back on the table because they no longer felt they were supposed to smuggle. (Some thought ONE Bible was too many!) I was caught off guard when one lady handed me her entire lot and informed me, "God told me not to smuggle any across." *This gives you a funny feeling for two reasons.* The rest of the people were trying to map out courses of action and exchange ideas of how to hide that many Bibles in such small bags. Nerves were taut. When we left the meeting room, the tables were empty of all the Bibles.

Working to try to fit all the extras in our small travel bags, Donna and I mulled over the best plan. We had one consensus—every Bible in *our* luggage meant one more person *in China* with a Bible. We made a decision that went against the grain of our gender: we decided not to take extra clothes, beauty paraphernalia or even our toiletries for the next three days in order to take as many Bibles as possible. It never crossed my mind to ask the Lord *if* we should take Bibles, just *how many*, and I couldn't get a clear answer on that. The realization that each Bible meant souls was all I thought about while packing. I slept well that night knowing this was the part of the trip for which I had been waiting.

CHAPTER FIVE
Border Smugglers

THERE IS NOTHING LIKE the feeling of private morning devotionals on the day you are smuggling Bibles into a Communist country. There is no apathy or sleepiness, only a sharp awareness of wanting to make sure that *if* God wanted to tell you anything *extra* that morning, you were ready to hear it. This is one of those remarkable days when, within 24 hours, you would know if you heard God or not. There would be less *middle ground* in your life today than on other days. The only emotion I remember is just wanting to get the day started.

In that early morning quietness, the Lord had assured Donna and me *our* Bibles would go through and there wasn't going to be a problem. Standing in the train station, the troops were talking and laughing, but it was an antsy company. Stories were whispered around of past years when ONE person had been caught and EVERYONE lost their Bibles. Individual blunders and unfortunate incidents had traumatized *whole* teams in the past.

Donna and I pondered the larger reality, "We don't want just our Bibles to go through, but all 2,000 of them." We had only received assurance on *our* Bibles. Suddenly, it felt as though we had the weight of the entire team's load on us as well and that our prayers had been much too narrow. The night before had felt so individualized, but now I had the stark realization the task would only be successful as a group effort.

Everyone kept making sure the group, especially the *louder* members, remembered the warnings from the last briefing: "You're tourists now, going into Communist China, so don't be saying, 'Praise the Lord' or 'Hallelujah,' or all the things we like to say."

A misfire happened, even before the action began. We were in Hong Kong's train departure station waiting for instructions to move when five men introduced themselves as our guides from mainland China. They began interrogating the team: "*What is this group? Who are you? Why have you gotten together? What is the purpose of your visit?*" One guy from our group couldn't think of what to say when they relentlessly quizzed us. For some reason this "barrage of questioning" has the same effect it does when a lawyer fires repeated questions at the person on the witness stand, until he breaks. After 10,000 warnings, this self-appointed spokesperson felt the need to explain, "Oh, we're just missionaries." He slipped up before we even got across one border! There was an unintended gasp. Did he just sign our death warrant? Quickly, we committed that blunder into the hands of the Lord.

We stepped on board a passenger train, which looked as though it was beyond a healthy retirement age. A sensation occurred like that of entering a time warp and we were being transported *back* in time.

It gave the team quite a case of the jitters as we rolled out of Hong Kong into the land of the Red Dragon. The sterile complexion reminded us we were uninvited visitors—with prison-like guardhouses and rolls of sharply barbed wire above the metal fence marking the spot where it changed from free soil to communist soil. Our train stopped so Chinese military soldiers could join us as an unexpected escort.

While the unfriendly border landscape cut the awareness deeper into our consciousness that we had just crossed into Communist Red China—the guns, the guards, and the security detail placed with us made us even more anxiously mindful that we were hiding something. The problem was: *were we hiding it well enough?* A group loaded down with 2,000 illegal Bibles with nothing more than light luggage to conceal the transport is very conspicuous to trained eyes. I processed the predicament; even if I had a sudden change of mind about smuggling, I was committed. There was no way to repack my luggage or to revamp my strategy; I would be matched with my luggage as soon as I exited the train and escorted to inspection. The next time our bags were opened would be in the presence of armed soldiers. So I cannot say that the train ride was relaxing. The anticipation of our first border smuggling still lay ahead.

It was sheer psychological torment to our minds as the music blasted out a metallic sound similar to a pitch of a thousand fingernails scraping a chalkboard of "Chiing, Chaing, Choing", and no volume control button. Hour after hour of pure, undisguised Chinese torture blared from their hidden speakers. We began trying to hang onto the shreds of our sanity as we felt it trying to slip away, listening to the over-volumed, ear-shrieking "music" against the rattle of the train on the tracks.

The panorama from the train, on the other hand, resembled a page from a National Geographic magazine glued to our window. The rice farmers still wore the old pointed hats made out of bamboo leaves as they bent over to toil in the patchwork of rice paddies. My face was super-glued to the window; my thoughts were transfixed by the ancient practice of farmers employing water buffalo to do the labor on endless rice fields and equally astounded by the complete absence of farm machinery. The past and present were simultaneously placed next to each other with no dividing line—a very primitive culture preserved like an archeological find within the borders of a modern world.

Rudely, I was jerked back to my world when a steely-eyed soldier strutted down the aisle, stopped and defiantly glared down at me before slapping a clipboard into my lap. It didn't take words for me to understand, I was required to sign this official document. I glanced through the pages. Instantly, I was faced with a moment for which nothing in my past religious upbringing had prepared me

—should I outright lie and say I had no religious materials in my luggage so the form could be used against me if we were caught? Or, *should I* answer that question directly and spill the secret that all *240 of us* were "smugglers" and were loaded down with *2,000 Bibles?* My Sunday School teacher had never addressed *what to do* in a situation like this.

This soldier had the appearance of a robot: an *armed* robot with the unblinking stare of a tiger who sought to intimidate me by the unspoken challenge of who would break eye contact first. I was being tested by this man. It was like he had singled me out for an old fashioned game of chicken—an assessment of nerves—*loser looks away first*, when we both knew the real game was truth or dare with much higher stakes.

His rigid appearance in a murky green uniform added to his imposing demeanor. He had sent me a curt, non-verbal, but CLEAR message. I had the feeling he had sized up the team, found the *youngest* and the *weakest* link—and put the intimidation screws down on me. *Did he suspect something?* I locked eyes with him, not *daring* to break eye contact...

With a bit of pleasure, I inwardly mused—*if this trip was being judged by never having a dull moment, God had certainly marked dull off the chart, and I was getting my money's worth.* I scanned the document as he hovered over me, almost *daring—even defying* me to sign. I let the pen lightly scratch through the portion of the document about "no Bibles" as if I accidentally grazed the paper; then *boldly* circled the part that I had no religious materials "detrimental to the Chinese Government or people" and carefully initialed those words. With much satisfaction, I signed my name across the bottom of the page and slapped the clipboard back into his hands, mimicking him. He spun around and with a huff, left without passing it off to another person in our compartment; nor did anyone else ever say they had to face this government form. I wondered later if they were suspicious or if this was routine to Westerners. When he and the paper had disappeared, everyone on the train near me looked startled that I had been chosen for that *little display* of Chinese hospitality.

My conscience was on sudden alert. Like a body part from which I had not suffered any previous sensations, it was now needing, wanting—almost demanding attention. Nevertheless, my spirit was settled and at peace. I reviewed the last few minutes of my life with the same unsettled emotion as that of having an exam thrust upon me for which I had not prepared, but had just finished. Inwardly, I felt secure that I had been both honest and shrewd.[28] I never realized I had a *conscience organ,* but he was hopping around on the inside now with more perceptible stimuli than when your heart skips a beat or your stomach ties a knot. I had done him justice, yet had not blown the whistle. Those Bibles were not detrimental, they were the best gift we could give to any Chinese person or foreign government. My conscience bore

---

[28] Matthew 10:16

witness that I served the law of a higher kingdom.[29]
So I settled back into the rice field scenery out the
dingy lace curtains, the edgy conversations on both
sides of us, the blaring music and my own thoughts,
anticipating what awaited us at the next stop.

It was on that train, in a deep moment of reflection,
I first sensed the **oneness** of the group. It is a defining
moment when individuals on a team become one with their
team. We had been gathered up from many different walks
of life, and yet, we had put ourselves in a position where we
were *in this* together. It didn't show on the surface, but it
was there, inside that train-car, we *united in purpose.*

The mood of the team was like a high-spirited
horse before the opening of the gate. We were giddy.
Perhaps, it was the peace of God, or perhaps it was
nerves, but everyone on the train was laughing, telling
silly jokes and being overly cheery. It definitely cast us
in our cover role of the *stereotypical*—slap-happy,
carefree American tourist.

I wore a pair of white capris, a pale blue polo shirt
(team members wouldn't have any trouble guessing
what I would be wearing each day), and a large camera
hung by its strap around my neck, in hopes of
completing my tourist ensemble. As I stepped off the
train, I kept telling myself: "Think *tourist.*"
We headed resolutely through the door into a room of
customs inspections, immigration, security checks,

---

[29] Acts 5:29

entrance applications, passport checks, military guards and uniformed police—only for me to want to recoil, back right out and regroup when I saw the thoroughness of the Chinese guards' inspection of their *tourists.* The army uniforms and the automatic weapons all made it like a surreal scene of Communist China. No one had to remind us, religion was unwelcomed. A resolute, singularity of quiet purpose descended upon the group.

If I had to write a definition for **fervent prayer,** two things come to mind: *First, it occurs* when you're going 20 miles over the speed limit—it's your fourth ticket, your parents have decreed that you must pay your own insurance and you see red and blue lights circling the interior of your car. *The other definition:* You are the next person in line for luggage inspection in Communist China and you are loaded down with Bibles!

Praying sounds more like begging: *repenting of sins you have never repented of before.   Hidden stuff you have previously been holding onto—you start openly telling God ALL about.* Donna and I were standing together confessing every conscious, thoughtless act in our young lives, pleading for our sins not to be remembered. I have one phrase I like to use on occasions like this: *"MERCY! Lord, have MERCY on me!"*

We were watching another group in front of us go through inspection, which was probably the wrong thing to do while trying to keep our faith built up. These men took every single embarrassing item out of the bags. *Mercy!* The guard's hands searched behind the lining. *Mercy!*

Foreigners who had **NO** Bibles on them were offended at how hostile the search was! I cautiously studied every line, searching for a guard who was not thorough. I could find no weak link. Our earlier confidence eroded. Every happy story Corrie ten Boom had written of smuggling, recounting "*blind*" communist inspectors, seemed like bedtime fairy tales right now. These men appeared to have X-ray vision. *Mercy!*

One smartly dressed European woman was irate while they were pulling the lining out of her suitcase, running their hands along the edges and dumping her precisely packed clothing items. It appeared the two men didn't care that they damaged a suitcase. She was having a meltdown, yet she clearly had nothing to hide. When the inspection was over, they made no attempt to put her garments back.

> There is nothing worse than facing a hostile inspection by an angry guard with an automatic weapon strapped on his back, *in your face* grilling you, shouting at you in a language you don't understand.

The guard took the stacks that had toppled over, threw them back in like a five-year-old's concept of packing and with no apologies, slammed the lid down with at least four inches of protruding clothing. It looked like the luggage had thrown up its contents. There is a strange phenomenon about watching the exchange between two people who don't know each other's language! Their volume gets louder and louder, as if that will break the language barrier! I could feel the lining in my stomach and my last meal.

Rationally, we calmed ourselves by noting our group leaders had been doing this now for eleven years. I assured Donna that they must know what they were doing. So I guess she ran to find out if I had made a viable observation. Donna loves questions and she can ask very pointed ones until she finds some inner satisfaction and stops. However it had the opposite effect. At this point, someone clarified that this organization had never brought Bibles in until two years ago. I might add that Donna was quite taken with this fresh piece of information she had unearthed and mumbled something about feeling a kinship to guinea pig dissections in anatomy lab. **Every logical crutch I could think of was evaporating.**

The team leaders were experimenting with our direct approach for future teams because of a past fiasco. The disaster occurred when one overly zealous lady put Bibles in her dress and portrayed herself as though she were pregnant. Right at the counter her belt busted loose and all the Bibles fell to her feet. The customs officers tore the group to smithereens that year and ripped their luggage to shreds. All Bibles were confiscated. Her unfortunate incident didn't just affect her: for every Bible seized, it meant one less home without a Bible.

This verified our suspicion that once one Chinese Bible was found the inspectors would seize the entire team's. As a whole, our team had packed Bibles similarly: we had only one small piece of temporary luggage—so, perhaps there was only one article of clothing in the luggage wrapped around our precious load of Bibles. I sat there analyzing the situation, realizing that all it took was opening ONE suitcase and the guards would be all over us. The first person caught, more than likely, meant the *whole* group was caught. *It suddenly seemed like an impossibility to get any across.*

> You ponder: "I can not believe I've gotten myself into this mess. 'Okay, who talked me into this?' Oh yeah, those Corrie Ten Boom books I used to read and her famous 'blind the eyes of the guard' prayer.[30] You try praying the famous 'LORD, make seeing eyes blind,' and you're looking at them—nothing happens, and you're next in line. For the first time in my life, I was thinking *ugly* thoughts about Corrie ten Boom and that book of hers I had read."

My mind started reeling off worst case scenarios—which are like invisible boundary lines to put worry in perspective. Churning imaginations: if we were caught, then *this could* happen, or *this...* It was like watching

---

[30] Corrie Ten Boom. **A Prisoner and Yet.** Chapter Four: Angels Round About Us, page 99.

movies with different endings in your head. I had always wanted to write for the Reader's Digest Book Section and thought this might give me my chance, if caught and locked in a Chinese jail.

All nervous mirth suddenly came to a standstill when I noticed the oldest couple on the team was in line directly in front of me. When he placed his arm around his wife's thin shoulders, I noticed he shook slightly, as older people do. Up close, I now, more than ever, admired the couple for traveling overseas, trying out new things. What struck me was the trusting, simple kind of way in his manner. They were both loaded with Bibles and I realistically feared they might not live through the jail sentences I had read about in China. They, just as I, had heard about the trip and also wanted to smuggle. What a contrast of nature between this couple and these hard, cruel border people. There was no flexibility to China's intolerance toward what they viewed as dangerous. The Chinese government's mentality was rigid in personality and rules, and smugglers came in all kinds of packages. The contrast of the young and old, the daring and fearful, yet we would all meet the same fate in a few minutes... *Only God knew what would happen next!*

Moving along in line gave me plenty of time to observe this older couple. Listening to the gentle conversation between the two of them, at an age when most elderly people have acquired more fears, they talked quietly about their faith. It sobered up my toying with *worst-case* scenarios and youthful yearnings for action. We were a team, and I desperately didn't want to watch any misery suddenly befall our older members.

The worst part of standing in line was the mental torture of watching other international groups have adverse reactions to the guards. The time the border guards put into each inspection reflects the Chinese mind's inclination to meticulous details and proved that these men weren't letting someone rush them past anything just because of time pressures. They weren't missing anything! The examinations were all the same—intimidating, ridiculously thorough and upsetting to travelers the world over. It made it harder to have any degree of faith. I don't know what I was thinking this morning when I put a few measly cotton balls on the top of the Bibles, believing that when the "blind", gun-toting guards un-zipped it, all they would see were my *innocent* cotton balls and promptly zip it back up and apologize for inconveniencing me. I guess that was about as deep as I was thinking this morning before I watched people being forcibly searched. These guards seemed part robot, part iron monster. If we were busted, they were more than capable of literally throwing the book at us—page by page!

I left the inspection line again to join a small group to pray **one more** time. Morning prayer had given me such confidence—I had actually been impatient for this moment to arrive. Suddenly, my entire prayer life didn't seem as thorough as it needed to be.

I tried *re-praying*! Words jammed in my throat.
Any more prayers stuck in my mouth. Then a strange
phenomenon happened; I could only sing my prayers,
and I can't sing. And I can't stand to be heard. Yet,
this moment beckoned and called for anything that
would get heaven's attention. Donna asked, "What are
you singing?" I retorted, "I'm going to write a thank
you note to Ivan Tait as soon as I get back," (because I
was singing his tune—*Let the peace of God have
preeminence).* Donna joined in on my feeble attempt
and people in the group began catching on and joining
in on singing the phrase with quite a bit of enthusiasm.

The time was ticking as we stayed out of the line,
trying to build up confidence that our whole group
would make it through without a disaster. "Lord,
You're going to protect our group." *But how?* All of
us had so little covering the *bread* in our luggage, and
my bag was bulging so badly. I had only had the room
to stuff cotton balls in the cracks. Regret seized me
that I had not applied more creativity in my packing in
Hong Kong and there was a good chance that after
this, I would never want to think of another cotton
ball. I usually had a back-up plan, but our options
were limited. It was like we were on an assembly line
conveyor belt headed in the direction of our inspectors
with nowhere to unload, nowhere to repack. I felt
brain locked. I couldn't even think of a plan in which I
could give God any ideas on how He could get us out
of this mess! With all honesty, it was impossible for

any of us to make it through the kind of inspection we were seeing. **So I just sang.**

Our impromptu group was about to adjourn and get back into line for the inevitable, when a petite Oriental man came over and asked to speak to our leader. He gave us the impression he was highly agitated. I was present when he made the announcement to us in broken English, "The station is much too full! Six trains! We cannot possibly inspect every one." He did that gesture of repeated, rapid bowing of the head with his hands cupped together in front of his chest, which is so typically Asian.

His mannerism was like he was asking our pardon, but his words were utterly shocking to our ears, "If it would not be an inconvenience to you, we will pass your group through without inspection!" How do you answer that? No one moved. No one uttered a sound. Everyone had incredulous looks on their faces because no one was completely sure we had heard him correctly.

He actually acted deeply disturbed that this suggestion might have perturbed us and apologized several times. Unlike this morning when one man said too much, now no one could think what to say. This unexpected favor he was asking from us almost erased our minds. Someone in our circle found enough composure to say, "Yes!", and with that, they gathered us up and marched us right past the customs desk. The inspectors looked as though they sensed something amiss and were on the verge of raising some objection but passed us through without either side daring to say anything more than necessary. As I neared the inspection counter, there was no doubt that one could feel the unspoken protest as the armed guards let us pass by without a clash. The inspector I had previously observed, eyed my passport then simply responded with a curt nod and waved me on. Team members filed forward, placed all luggage on the table, and showed these very tense guards our passports. I watched as the armed men passed **all 240 people through without opening any of our team's luggage or confiscating any** *bread!*

I went outside I knelt down and this Texan kissed Communist China's soil with heart-felt gratitude. I repeated many times over, "Thank You, Lord," and "Hallelujah" before I got up off my knees! I knew God had been with us. *Every Bible made it into the country.*

The music I was now hearing in my head sounded more like Handel's *Hallelujah Chorus* and the angels were singing backup. Never had I felt such a swing of emotions in a twenty-four hour span.

I had thought for sure I was going to see the inside of a Chinese jail rather than continuing on as a tourist. From this moment forth, China never felt communist to me again; I was going to be able to move about freely.

CHAPTER SIX

China by Day

SMUGGLING WAS OVER FOR us after daring to attempt to take 2000 Bibles through the border inspection. God had made our entire mission trip extremely successful and we had a great deal over which to rejoice and now we could relax. We had passed through without any unfortunate incidents and without any detection. When we arrived at our hotel we would place our *bread* in a designated room. The challenging phase of our mission trip was behind us; and personally, my favorite aspect of the trip had just concluded, but *what a story!* My mind ran through the details of the last narrow escape. For the rest of the trip we could take it easy as tourists exploring an ancient, exotic land or, so I thought...

From our tour bus window we could view the main city.[31] The rural areas we saw earlier from the train looked as primitive as it did from when time began, but from the bus the city looked like we had stepped onto a Hollywood set of early 1900s. There was so little progress. I asked our guide, "Where did this style of architecture come from?" (They looked anything but Asian in design.) She replied, "The British and

---

[31] Several have published their story with names, places and dates but I will leave the name of the city off for security purposes.

French built them similar to the style of architecture you have in New Orleans." Her comparison with something familiar to us made her knowledge impressive. Someone else asked, "What kind of progress has China had?" This young college guide went on to explain, "A year ago private individuals were given the opportunity to buy cars." Among the heavy bicycle population, I counted about 25 cars on the road. "Which," she continued, "very few have the money to buy." A man who had been in the Orient four years before leaned over and inserted, "There were absolutely no cars on this road when we were here last trip." China was delighted with her progress.

As far as we were able to observe, having a business with employees meant having someone working beside you, selling little trinkets or produce. Vendors dotted the main road. My eyes studied a man selling watermelons on the street and laughed when I saw he was eating a slice of his own product. Instead of street lamps, he had rigged a single dangling light bulb so he could work at night. I looked at the simple people and thought of the *bread* we had. When the Scripture says that *the poor have the Gospel*, it explained why it was only *simple* people like these who would get the Bibles. The government and state officials rejected them. It occurred to me that these poor people were blessed because they were ignored and the government wasn't paying much attention to the gifts we brought to "the poor".

The guide was eager to explain how China had become Westernized, and she believed they would embrace democracy in the near future.[32] She noted, for example, the increased curiosity of university students about the West. She was enthusiastic about the changes and eager to exchange ideas with us. These Chinese young people were intelligent, engaging and hungry for Western thought. I didn't sense a resistance to our way of life, only a longing for it.

"The only *new* construction in this city is the hotel where you have reservations. It was built to please the Westerners," our guide commented. She laughed, "International dignitaries are lodged there." The comment was an off-handed way of building our aspirations and flattering our egos. On a more somber note she added, "And with the expanse of shops under one roof you will have no need to leave the premises to shop." Was it a sales plug or a warning?

The softer gender heard only one word in her sentence—"shop!" Husbands were discussing budgets with uninterested wives, who, in turn, were ready to pounce on the convenient, hotel-housed retail shops our female guide had used to entice us as we exited the bus. As the team proceeded toward check-in, the women in our party did not take time for the formality

---

[32] This was several years before the massacre in Tiananmen Square of freedom fighting Chinese students. Her prophecy was to take longer than either of us thought to fulfill, if it ever happens at all.

of checking in or unpacking before sprinting for the expansive indoor shopping mall.

Its standards were far beyond anything I had ever seen. There was a lobby with engineered waterfalls pouring into lazy streams containing brightly colored fish nestled in a rainforest paradise. Being raised in a rural community, I was enthralled with the exotic fish in the midst of it. The designers had definitely captured the idea of self-contained, so there was no logical reason for us to have to leave the building.

Our personal rooms had all the conveniences of the American home. The view from our balcony overlooked a river that swarmed with local activity. I was startled at the contrast below on the streets. The Western Christians stayed in these posh hotels with lavish lifestyles: food and drinks, massages, and immoderate luxuries—and they never looked out the window to the persecuted church.

As a 22-year-old, I saw what looked to me like lukewarmness and outright compromise at the higher rungs. Yet, the 240 lay people seemed eager, sincere and temperate, while not requiring much accountability from their leadership. Each culture has produced its own brand of Christianity. *Westernized* Christian tradition insisted on insulating herself from anything that would rock her carefully guarded comfort zones.

The extravagant living quarters served us well as part of "the cover" for this trip—lavish tourist by day and no one would suspect that by night the underground church would meet with us in this kind of luxury. So, I made no attempt to crusade against our indulgences since it served a useful purpose in distracting attention from our real mission. But I made an inner commitment not to live a lifestyle that insulated me from the very people I wanted to reach.

What the husbands could not restrain in their wives, these strict Chinese guides could. It was obvious we would not be let out of the Chinese hosts' sight for one second over the next three days. The hospitality and polite courteousness was only a mask for keeping the group *managed*—underhand and under control. Our team would be meticulously following the itinerary and *agendas* they had typed and handed to us. They were determined to provide Western visitors well-orchestrated presentations of how *beautiful*, how *talented* and how *free* China was. The propaganda was in full swing from the moment we arrived. They desperately wanted us to go home telling our friends how badly we had misjudged China and that there was very little difference between communism and what we had in a "democratic society". In fact, they had already *proven* to us they could build hotels comparable to the best America had.

First stop, we visited the zoo where the guide exuded great pride in what he explained was their *rare* black swan. We walked forever past empty cages to find this swan at the back of the zoo enclosure. Two hundred Americans demonstrated little reaction to what was considered a great rarity. Next, we were on a foot safari looking for the panda bear. The Chinese method of hosting a tour of a zoo was making our team find the animals *in the wild* ourselves. Were they stalling?

The Chinese host gave a prolonged, no nonsense speech about the Chinese presenting an American zoo with its first panda. It seemed the lengthy speech paralleled the filibuster techniques of a U.S. legislator on the floor of the Senate who employed a *similar type* of Chinese torture—talking you to death. The guides could eventually wear down your sanity, and I gathered that their philosophy was similar to my mom's—if she repeats herself enough, a person would eventually agree with her. In reality, the caged animals looked miserable—as *cramped,* as *stifled,* and as *colorless* as their human counterparts in the city.[33] How different Taiwan was in this respect from China.

The panda looked extremely bored in the sterile cage with heavy steel bars. He never stirred; his head never lifted up from the concrete floor to see that he had visitors. It wasn't that *he* was disappointing, it was that he looked like they had stolen all his beauty from him in this very controlled environment.

---

[33] Taiwan (chapter 2) looked like a Chinese version of San Francisco. The people themselves, not just the officials, flourished economically.

Just as we were departing, the animal that captured the Americans interest was their impolite gorilla. It was amazing what he found in his cage to throw at us visitors as we passed. Quite a crowd built as we waited for someone else to be under attack as each unsuspecting target walked past his cage. Hidden group members roared with laughter at their surprise. The puzzled Chinese guides could not understand how the Americans seemed more enthralled with this coarse and badly behaved beast than with all the hoopla about the swan and the panda.

After our long walk, it was time for a refreshing snack in a Chinese eatery. I don't know what we were expecting—a bakery, an ice cream shop, a candy store... But its counters and glass shelves were stocked with roots and greens and portions of animals from which to choose a snack. What fascinated me was the dried, flying lizard piled up like donuts on display. First of all, I didn't know they weren't extinct, and secondly, I thought surely this was a place to purchase specimens for biology lab. I sought out my ever helpful guide to ask about this prehistoric-looking platter of lizards behind glass. Instead she went over to the owner to place my order in Chinese and told me the price. I asked this young, educated college girl, "How would I get it home?" She exclaimed, "Oh, it is a delicacy to eat!" Sheltered behind me, Donna, with a hand on each of my shoulders for support was entering a state of semi-conscious shock. These missionary food tales went past any imagination or category she had reserved for the trip, and at this point, I think she wanted out of the competition. I was intrigued with what the Chinese found to be appetizing[34].

Our pretty and pert guide went on to explain how the Chinese would sit with Western businessmen around a table with a hole in the middle in which they would place a live monkey, hack-saw off the crown of the monkey's head, place straws in his brain and partake like they were sharing a soda. She commented that it was quite expensive for the Chinese to provide their guests with this delicacy. I did a double take—to see if she was doing what we do to strangers in Texas. However, the Chinese don't appear to jest (and this one seemed especially sober). Donna was having digestion ills just hearing me probe her with questions. What worried me was a deeper philosophical issue: the Chinese had a much more brutal irreverence for life than the Westerner's conscience. Vulnerability is a funny feeling—to knowingly put yourself at risk in a culture that shares very few, if *any*, of your values. We loaded the bus, with very few of us buying any snacks.

As our bus honked at the people cycling I took note that personal individuality was not encouraged here. Everyone wore the same white cotton hat—and our bus, not to be outdone, joined the ranks of conformity and purchased one—so we'd be the only person back home

---

[34] ...but not to the point of eating it.

with one! Family life appeared thoroughly wholesome with large families peddling together down tree-lined streets. Staring out my window and soaking in the simple scenery, I couldn't help but be appalled at a graphic billboard we suddenly passed. It showed each stage of development of the baby in the mother's womb and then the baby being terminated in the final picture block. I assumed it publicized a vivid appeal against abortion.

I questioned our female guide because I was puzzled by these government pro-life billboards, openly advertising this horror, to curtail abortion. She matter-of-factly explained, "Oh, no, China is not pro-life. The message is telling our people that if they conceive more than the one child limit or if they are disappointed in the child's sex that there are means of disposal. The billboard *encourages* them to abort!" I looked again at the sign. It was appalling that China would unabashedly show what a graphic procedure abortion of a child is; American sentimentalities would **never** allow such a sign to go up in the streets.[35] However, China showed the details to *promote* abortion.

I realized that the Chinese mind, under communism, has no respect for life at any level. What

[35] American morality and sentimentality and respect for a person's feelings would never show such a ghastly sight of the brutality of an abortion! What would turn any stomach is just merely advertising the one child policy for the Chinese. China's blatant lack of respect for life was shockingly repulsive; then it came like a moment of truth, for the hypocrites that we, as Americans are. The only difference I could see: Americans do it and conceal it. China flaunts it.

made me think they would value *my life* if anything went wrong? *They didn't value their own!* (How different from the Filipino, who, in a later trip, had jumped in front of me and shoved me out of the way of an oncoming bus.) Neither the conditions at the zoo, nor the monkey story, nor the abortion billboard showed any innate compassion for the Chinese soul; instead, it indicated the hardness we might expect if their displeasure turned on us.

We attended an acrobatic production, which impressed me with the Chinese culture's disciplined talent. It was an amazing display of balance and coordination, the result of years of practice. Young children and adults alike produced mind-boggling feats of strength and rhythm as they juggled human bodies, small children, furniture, glassware, etc. Anything not bolted down ended up in midair.

Buddhist temples were also on the list. By this juncture of the trip, God had delivered me of my prejudice and the Oriental Christians had endeared themselves to me; however, the Oriental gods were neither on my 'good' nor 'want to see' list! My prejudice was warranted against the Buddhist religion and I did not want to visit the temple of foreign gods for tourist reasons.[36]

Towering over us, a statue of a large unsmiling Buddha cast a shadow over our bus. I was shocked that the vast majority of our team had no qualms against this

---

[36] I draw the line between entertainment motives and missionary causes.

kind of sight-seeing and didn't even remember to pray specifically for protection over themselves in places that are temples for the worship of demons.[37] I think Donna and I were the only two who stayed on the bus, and the guide found our refusal disconcerting. The team that came back to the bus was not the same playful group that had left. They were incensed at what they encountered. Stories were told of how roughly they were treated by Buddhist monks who attempted to coerce these *Westerners* to participate in various steps of pagan purification and veneration. The Americans were looking for entertainment and the Chinese attempted to give them an education. The result wasn't a pretty mix.

~

When I saw the State Church, I was floored at the surface rituals and superficiality of the service. What a contrast between it and the real Church that I would see later that night with my very own eyes. The flexibility would have been humorous if it had not been so disturbing. *How could one not question the*

---

[37] Jesus did not ignore spiritual battles, but armed Himself with the Word. He could have just said, "I am the Son of God, this is only the devil, so I will just ignore him." However, as our example, He did not ignore, but resisted. We have the Greater One in us, but this is not a fact of presumption, but one of equipping.

Also, I cannot picture Jesus in His three years of earthly ministry joining in on tours of pagan temples. If He used a whip in His own temple, I wonder if He would view the world as under His authority also, and take drastic measures against open forms of idolatry. Either way, He wasn't ever on educational tours, but on ministry purposes.

So the rule of thumb I have used since then is: go in such places only to accomplish a specific God-given mission. See I Corinthians 10: 20

credibility, when the schedule of services was changed repeatedly for our whimsical convenience? When it was convenient for us, the service could be *arranged,* probably in every sense of the word, by our guides. The whole ritual struck me as peculiar. First, the service itself was rearranged on a weekday at an afternoon hour—it was long and in Chinese; the audience was a handful of elderly Chinese people scattered throughout the pews who openly slept through the music and preaching.

Secondly, the choir wore shorts underneath their robes rather than church attire. At the end of the service they had an apparent call to the front where a few came forward. Ushers handed the congregation books we were told were Bibles. The guides were very proud of this fact and told us there was a misunderstanding in the West that *the Church* in China couldn't have Bibles. Afterward, I watched them take back the Bibles. What shocked me was not that the Chinese insisted they have freedom of religion like America, but that the Americans on the trip were so gullible. The message the officials seemed to want us to believe is, *"Don't bring us Bibles, we have too many of our own!"*

I spent much time just listening to our group's opinions, since I was one of the youngest. Several among our team totally revised their idea of the Chinese policy on the freedom of religion, based on this *one* service, even though we never knew one word that they said, or understood one song that they sang, or could decipher one word on the pamphlets that they handed out. On the bus, one man remarked that he was going to tell his friends back home how China had churches *just like ours.*[38]

Chinese are very motivated to exhibit a good appearance and Americans are very good at believing appearances. It is a lethal combination. Jesus told his followers to be as wise as serpents and as harmless as doves. One way or another Christians have contorted that to read—be as *mean as snakes and have the brains of a bird.* Sometimes I wondered how God got anything done with his bird-brain workers. I leaned my head against the window on the bus pondering what I had just witnessed: the methods of the Chinese and the mentality of Americans—like Eddy Haskell tutoring Gomer Pyle.

I think only when I saw the contrast of another culture, could I really begin to understand my own.[39] Although labels often are frustrating and restricting, having variations of styles and methods, and smorgasbords of valid ministries can be a positive sample of FREEDOM of CHOICE—and this country had few options. In this city, their choice was glaringly narrow—the State Church, a Buddhist Temple or the pressure of a life with the illegal church.

---

[38] There may be more truth to that than we would like to admit!

[39] In America, much is said about our divisiveness and fragmented church because we have so *many* different approaches. However, with the perspective of what we were seeing in China, the multi-variations give us a wider selection of choices on the menu.

Now it was time to get down to business about the *Number One* thing on our agenda. To no avail, we waited for someone to tell us what to do with our Bibles. Donna and I understood that 7:30 was our departure time for dinner and we had to be loaded on the bus for authentic Chinese food. We were killing time unpacking and hiding our *bread*. I had talked directly with people from previous teams and knew this hotel was famous for room checks during this dinner hour. We had no extra *stuff* in our luggage, so we plastered the room with random items that weren't nailed down. *Where could anything really be hidden in this room?*

I put my Bibles under the bed in a disguise with the bed skirt and a curtain. The way Chinese search— there was no place to hide. Donna put her batch under the mattress more than once, then changed her mind. She worked like a tornado in motion and it was better that I stand back and admire the progress. The fun was in the hunt—I had seen Donna in this mode before when she demonstrated as much flair in shopping, dessert buffets and other realms of women's prerogatives. I offered her some suggestions for where to hide her stash, but she thought my suggestions were unimaginative. Changing her mind frequently aided the eventual satisfaction level.

I busied myself with other important matters. While she was having a mental meltdown over her dilemma, I stood up on the bed and talked into the light fixture socket. Next, I searched over the picture frame on the wall. I settled in on the lamp, "Hey, you Communists, this is Angelia Kay Ruth. You need to loosen up." Then I would preach to them. Donna asked me indignantly, "What on God's green earth are you doing, they told us the rooms were bugged!" Ignoring her quick criticism and slow perception, I retorted, "Exactly my point, I am evangelizing the guy stationed to listen to the activity in our room!"

I was hoping the man they had placed in charge of monitoring us understood my articulate *Texas* English as I lectured him on areas where he might need improvement. Winston Churchill couldn't have said it better, speaking to the Germans. While most were afraid of some unknown spy eavesdropping, I saw it as a positive opportunity to be listened to! My philosophical rhetoric, I think, gave Donna time to repeatedly decide where she would hide her stockpile, as frequently as women do with any major decision. Donna's stash ended up in cabinet drawers, in our bags, under the mattress—"a little everywhere" was her last conclusion. For a grand finale, we booby-trapped the room to know if we were searched—we laid objects in certain ways over our luggage, and Donna strategically placed a strand of hair on top of the disarray to determine if they tampered with our things. *There was method to our madness.* Afterward, we then ransacked our own room; hoping perhaps they would think we had done *the search* for them!

A terse phone call came from the lobby interrupting our project, "Hurry up. Where are you? The bus is leaving now." The Chinese have a distaste for tardiness.

We ran for the door, only to find out the lock on our room door didn't work. How were we to lock our Bibles in our room? There were two guards who watch each hall, and Donna took it upon herself to *go inform them* that our door wouldn't lock. This complication created a double jeopardy. This was either the best solution ever or the most stupid thing we had done. Had a rash decision only made a bad situation that much worse?

In order to distribute the mounting pressure evenly and to make sure Donna was as upset as I was, I listed out our escalating problems to her as we departed:
- our Chinese guide is angry at the two of us
- the fleet of buses are all loaded except for us
- there was nowhere to honestly hide anything in this room
- earlier our friends had delivered their "bundles"
- and now, for Pete's sake, the door won't lock![40]

I am stunned—it had gone from bad to worse in seconds. It made it so much more complicated to have growing numbers of Chinese security people around our *wide open* door, trying to fix our non-working lock for a room loaded with Bibles, while we left.

---

[40] Doors and locks were a consistent problem for us: constantly leaving our keys in our door at night (3x), bellmen using their own keys to enter, and now we were given a room with a door which wouldn't lock.

Our miffed Chinese guide took the two stragglers and the restless team to the restaurant. I can't think of anything much more embarrassing than to be the last ones to board a bus; random remarks and teasing taunted us as we scurried to a seat, but we were too preoccupied to honestly care. I hoped someone could slip us some information on why our Bibles weren't picked up and what we were to do now. Everybody was whispering their story of depositing their *bread* and how excited they were that the smuggling was a complete success. The drop-off rooms were empty and the underground church had left! Of all things, women told accounts of being approached by strangers while they were shopping and told the exact location to take their *bread!* I was dumbfounded. We had purposely not gone shopping with everyone else to ensure we didn't miss whoever it was who would call us for our "bread!" I guess we had let down our guard when we made it across the border with our hoard of Bibles. It had been so miraculous and glorious to get all the Bibles through customs only to face the devastation of failing and being caught at this point. I feared it wasn't a team joke, I was the team's weakest link since I had utterly botched the simplest aspect of our assignment—we had missed our final instructions.

A second-year veteran told us a mission horror story that traumatized us. We had confided in him our fear of what we left in our room and he offered us no consolation. "The room searches are not a rumor.

Last year a woman walked into her room and there were three communist guards methodically going through her luggage, tearing everything to shreds. She had forgotten something, and when she walked in the room they just filed out and didn't say a word to her. That year all the rooms had been searched and the luggage gone through while everyone was at dinner," he informed us, candidly, with first-hand information. This dialogue ended abruptly as we were ushered into a local restaurant, but inside my head the conversation kept going. I couldn't quit pondering, "Of course, a mattress would be the first place they'd look."

There we were at our first dinner in China and I remember the table conversation revolved around the menu, with everyone fussing over the orange soda, served hot out of the can with no ice. It was like I was in another world, like one who was under water and hearing muffled voices on the surface complaining over *three days of only orange soda and no ice!*

My reality was of a different nature. I kept going over and over in my mind that scene of those men we left repairing the lock—the only room that still had Bibles. I suddenly lost my nerve, "Donna, let's get a taxi. I'm going back to make sure they're not searching our room." I looked to Donna for reassurance. Donna's mind wasn't any calmer—she described her condition to me with one word, "Petrified!"

Perhaps the situation was so uncanny we decided to turn the mess over to God. For some reason it seems to be easier to have faith when it gets ridiculous. Impossible situations appear to be His specialty:

> The two of us prayed, *"Lord, You didn't bring us this far to let us down. You didn't bring us across the border to let those Bibles get into the wrong hands. We have many people back home praying so we're just going to stand in faith for You to take care of this. You have promised angels who will guard us, so no one will find our Bibles..."*

We finished our prayer by both of us verbalizing out loud that we trusted Him.

It would be an understatement to say Donna and I couldn't wait to get back to our room. The suspense was terrible and the bus seemed to take three lifetimes returning us to our hotel. The hall was very quiet, considerably different from how we left it. Finding the door locked and requiring our key, it was obvious they had fixed "that problem" for us. Panicking I threw open the door. Instinctively, we rushed in and looked at all our hiding spots finding all the *bread* still there.

Donna had an expression of both tears and joy. The room had the appearance a tornado had struck, yet everything was exactly as it should be. I chuckled, "Donna, *not one* of our booby traps has been altered; but **neither** did the maid **clean up the mess!"** Donna burst out with a hearty chortle. Her infectious laughter at my dry humor always made me feel clever, which endeared her to me—and I *admired* her discriminating taste.

# CHAPTER SEVEN

At the Right Place ... At the Right Time

"YOU TWO ARE THE only ones on the team who didn't get your *bread* delivered!" One of our fellow Texas teammates slipped me this information in the hall as she was turning in for the night. Another lady whispered, "Oh, yes, the underground church has left!" We were deep into China and what we so carefully smuggled in seemed useless. We felt as rejected as two girls with corsages sent to us for the prom, but no one ever came to pick us up. What we achieved earlier seemed worthless! Exhausted teammates gratefully prepared for bed after a long, intense day of touring and after-dinner shopping in hotel gift stores while Donna and I sat on our piles of Bibles staring at each other and wondering what went wrong. It was probably our egos which were so deflated that we had been the only ones we knew who were skipped, but we couldn't decide how to fix our problem.

You can't ask questions like: *Who is the pick-up boy? What does the underground church look like? Could we call them? And what do we do with these Bibles if they never come for them? Will we be the only ones who get to smuggle Chinese Bibles **OUT** of China?* I was having vain imaginations, but this time in reverse: *trying to smuggle* Bibles in my luggage *back* *out of* the train station. We felt totally left out of the loop—one united, ecstatic team, and then the two of us!

Alarmed that the underground church had come and gone and we had missed the pickup completely, we went into action: one of us stayed by the phone, while the other one sniffed around for more information. Charlene's information[41] was important because it motivated us to research the matter further. If our Bibles had been picked up on schedule, we would have gone to bed like everyone else; and *without ever knowing what we missed,* it would have meant us passing up the most profound part of our experience— and the very thing that was going to impact our lives forever. It is good to know sometimes the supernatural does not *look* supernatural at the time.

For Donna and me to be some of the few who were missed does not appear to be a very significant detail of our story. Yet it grew increasingly exasperating. It was very trying on our nerves to be just sitting for hours in our room by the phone. Minute by minute we thought this part of our trip would be written off as a totally disorganized blunder, instead it was the method by which God brought us to the place where He wanted us and allowed us to do something that few people in the world ever get to do. This delay, although it made us feel utterly incompetent, proved very much to be the guidance of the Lord.

---

[41] Charlene was a fellow Texan and the only other person we knew before we began the trip. Her help and regular reports kept us from giving up and going to bed.

The phone, which we had stared at for so long, suddenly rang. It startled us, I think because we had begun to believe it wasn't working in the country. The voice on the other line gave us our coded instructions to take the *bread* to a particular room. We gathered it up, relieved that, at last, we had an answer—only to realize we had another set of immediate problems.

No one gives you directives for these sorts of things. If the nature of your personality requires staying in control and having immediate answers to questions, foreign mission trips will give you a mental collapse. We were learning quickly there were no information booths built into these operations and we had to do our own problem-solving in high-risk situations. With two armed people on each hallway watching everything you do, we did not want to arouse suspicions. It is not like a *Holiday Inn* where you are greeted with a friendly smile, a wave, and an UNARMED desk clerk who asks, "Is there anything I can do to help you?" Just passing the wary hotel men stationed in the hall was beyond difficult.

Donna navigated and I followed as we moved the *bread* to the elevator and then to the designated room (which happened to be the room of a friend of ours). A few scattered people came in with more *bread* as the clock neared the midnight hour. What an interesting mix of people in those rooms. One man privately narrated for us the basic system of transportation, "There is much movement of the *bread*—first to one room, only to be transferred to another and another, and so forth, just to confuse the situation so that there is not *too* much activity in any given room." The entire lot of Bibles then ended up in the room where connections were made between all parties involved. It was very tedious and time consuming but a sneaky little process that made us Americans feel *like extras* on a *Mission Impossible* episode.

"*Connections*" brought in from Hong Kong were secretly working in conjunction with the underground church. Both groups were rhythmically, but swiftly, packing luggage like factory workers. However, *the Hong Kong connections* alone had the assignment of moving the Bibles out of the hotel to the appointed destination. Donna and I were stunned when we ended up in the final room with the final group.

I remember incredibly mixed emotions, aching with everything in me to stay and watch the most amazing scene, but at the same time feeling overly conscientious— did our presence add any pressure or danger to this mission? We were assured by the leadership we were welcome to stay and watch the final process.

Donna's fun-loving drive and momentum[42] had worked us up through 240 team members and put us on a jovial first-name basis with Paul,[43] who had organized this operation. I have often thought if Donna had not desired to go on this trip with me,

[42] Donna' dives in head first and decides if she can swim afterwards.
[43] Name altered for the sake of the security of the operation.

possibly, I never would have ended up in the middle of all the action that night. Up until this point, we had been a comedy team with my playing the straight and Donna playing the stand-up comedienne who was never at a loss for words. Not only was Donna incredibly enjoyable, her actions were unintentionally strategic in the events that took place this night. What had only appeared a complementary personality blend originally now revealed the Divine Hand had matched us together from the start of this trip for this very moment. It was like a palatable state of surreal awe both inside of me and in the room that God had allowed us to be *the only two* members of the team[44] who were beholding what most people only read about.

Our attention was captivated by a teenager who had a fish emblem with an English inscription *One Way Up* on his T-shirt—briskly, yet very methodically, packing Bibles. I remember his hands were trembling, as he swiftly shuffled the Bibles into luggage for transport. An interpreter aided me in asking this 16-year old, "What would happen if you got caught tonight?" His slight smile gave us the impression he was glad that someone asked, yet he replied matter-of-factly, "They would kill the Chinese." I reeled from the gravity of his situation. I asked secondly, "What would happen to any one of the Americans?"

---

[44] With the exception of our Chinese member of the group.

He looked up. "They will put you in jail," he answered, as his hands picked up speed.

The adventurous excitement in my heart melted into something more serious. I thought about my previous, youthful speculation, "If we get caught and jailed, my Texas friends will come bust us out or I could always write for a major magazine about our prison experience in China!" But suddenly, it wasn't the same. *I had seen real faces, scared faces— teenagers packing Bibles* and no longer did I entertain the notion of letting ourselves get caught for any reason.

If we made a mistake, we would endanger many lives. As Americans, we have not lived under the fear and intolerance of an oppressive government, and times have not hardened us, so we are sometimes quite *idealistic, ignorant,* and *sloppy* in our overseas work. Apparently, I couldn't feel fear until I realized that my actions could endanger someone else. **I don't know if you have ever had a sensation in which you feel yourself grow up, but at that moment I felt myself cross some invisible growth-line.** When I saw real danger, I felt a little foolish for my earlier, childish horseplay in our hotel room of antagonizing any planted eavesdroppers. This teenage boy's childhood had been totally different from mine. There was a certain rawness to his reality. War makes adults out of children, and persecution eradicates immaturity out of us. In this short encounter, a reflection on his life imparted some maturity to me, and perhaps his realization, that we cared enough to come to his country to help, instilled in him hope and courage. In underground work, the adults were expected, but it was **the teenager** I met who impacted me. This experience highlighted my awareness that youth can reach youth.

The fear was visible in the room. I had never observed tension so thick that you could *see the abstract* with the naked eye. Each time someone would come to the door, people who otherwise expressed no emotion would involuntarily jump in unison. Illegal Bibles were all around us in half packed luggage. If any hotel employee or guard or policeman walked in for any reason or suspicion, everything about the operation was out in the open and there was nowhere to hide. This was a very vulnerable point in the process. Everyone suffered a severe case of the jitters. There was a tangible sense of danger in the air around these workers, so we prayed and interceded for their wisdom the entire time we were in the room. These were selfless members of the body of Christ who were willing to give their lives to help reach their people.

A beautiful Chinese Canadian named Maryann, whom we had been privileged to spend time with earlier, in less stressful circumstances, blended right in with the activity in the room. She was a recent convert from Buddhism, and her husband was yet to be saved.

She explained that she had been recruited, "Angie, because I'm Chinese and I will blend in with the people, tonight, they're going to allow me to take the Bibles to an arranged place." I was immediately envious of her assignment.

Abruptly, she pulled off one of the two shirts she had layered together and placed it in my hands. She gave me specific instructions with the bestowal, "If I make it back alive for breakfast, I want you to give this back to me. If I don't, I want you to kiss my daughter for me and tell her..." Her voice broke into subdued sobs that caught the rest of her words in her throat.

Like a man who rallies his last words before his ultimate departure, she declared boldly, "I'll do anything my Lord calls me to do." Then, between a few light sobs she pleads with me, "Will you pray for me?" I assured her she was covered in prayer: "Not only am I praying for you, but my church in Brownwood is praying twenty-four hours a day for these three days." I laid the shirt over my shoulder before I prayed. Perhaps I was a stand in for her daughter, for she repeatedly and tearfully kissed me.[45] Then she left the packing area. Joe,[46] another American Chinese director, interjected a little more light-heartedly, "If I don't come back, just give my stuff to Triple-A-Rental." We marched the pair out the

---

[45] Isn't God's sense of humor hilarious? Unconsciously, I had a fear of Chinese people before this trip, especially connected with Buddhism. Since God delivered me, I now have many close Chinese friends with this as a background!
[46] Names altered for the security of the operation.

hotel room door. Clutching the bags of *bread,* the two disappeared down the hall and slipped into the unknown of what lay ahead.

Paul was occasionally translating back and forth, so we caught bits and pieces of the underground workers' growing distress: "Girls, they simply aren't getting the Bibles out as quickly as they need to." Several times we raised the question, "We don't want to be in the way... Shall we leave?" Yet, in our hearts, both of us were screaming, "We don't want to leave!"

Donna and I privately discussed whether our presence added any danger to them. Strangely, we both felt impressed to stay. It was past midnight and the activity in the room moved in double time as speed, as never before, was of the essence; yet, almost as if on some invisible cue, the underground workers stopped their work. They evidently had not met their deadlines, realized it collectively and could not determine what they should do next.

"If you need anyone to help carry out the Bibles, we are offering our services," we proposed a second time. Again, it sounded like a stupid offer when it came out, but we had to at least offer our help when Paul reiterated that they were not transporting the Bibles out quickly enough. When Mary Ann had left earlier, the consensus of everyone involved was that no one else could be utilized. Two American girls, in the middle of China, in the dead of the night, are an unusual prospect for any type of undercover operation.

There was not a remote chance we would be included. Yet, we wanted to go with them so desperately we would have begged. Guilt and adrenaline were conducting a war inside of me. I understood; under no circumstances would it be worth it to risk this since light-haired Caucasians would stand out like a fox trying to hide with the hens.

Whatever was translated initiated an immediate outbreak of excited, animated talk among the workers. The next thing we knew, Paul asked us in English, "Who is stronger?" Donna and I about *killed each other* trying to prove ourselves the better fit. Perhaps, knowing we would never forgive the winner, Paul gave permission for the both of us to go. I was stunned when I heard it. If we had just been being polite to offer, we would have been in big trouble about now! Honestly, I don't think I could have been any happier. I was deeply elated and whispered, "Thank You, Jesus" and "Sorry, Mom"[47] ☺ under my breath.

We were a nice-looking, conspicuous pair for twelve-thirty at night. I slipped my departed friend's shirt over mine. Outfitted and ready to go! But when I looked down, I surprised myself—I was barefoot!

---

[47] Parents probably have the most difficult role in being back in the states while they know their children are involved in activities with the persecuted church. Can you imagine my mom and dad's prayer life each night as they thought about their child taking Bibles illegally into a Communist country? I smiled as I thought about the intensity of their prayers together, each night of these three weeks, before they went to bed. Mission Motto: Keep your parents on their knees!

I don't know what the proper attire is for smugglers, but I feared if I said something they might disqualify me instantly. Yet, on the other hand, I might cause added problems if anyone noticed I had no shoes on. They were already packing us down to send us off when I gathered my courage and blurted out, "Do I need shoes to smuggle?" Determined I would go barefoot before I let them nix me, I braced for their reaction. Like the timing was rehearsed, the three of them paused and lowered their eyes to look at my feet. Paul's expression was incredulous. Suddenly recalling my country upbringing, he sputtered out with a half-knowing smirk, "No! Well...? Go get them. Quick!"

My heart was beating so fast, I couldn't quit thinking—*the most thrilling thing I've ever done in my whole life is about to happen.* It felt like a lifetime of Christmases at once. In this room something had grown up inside of me. What had started out in my soul as a youthful mixture—a personal passion for adventure combined with certain elements of a divine calling with higher end purposes—transitioned into fervor, what I would almost describe as a burning for the things of God. I was known as a notorious practical joker and had organized some elaborate pranks, but I was finally involved in something with a constructive end to it. I liked high risk situations, but now there was purpose.

Many this night were afraid for their lives. However, when we suddenly had been included in the operation, we did not absorb any personal tension. This room had palpable fear in it, but Donna and I felt no fear whatsoever—despite increased personal jeopardy because we were without the support from a large team and were actively transporting Bibles with our own hands to Chinese people deeper into the heart of China. Unlike the nerve-wracking tension of the train station we experienced earlier today, there seemed to be a pervading blanket of peace over us and joy unspeakable.

As I left quickly to get the shoes, I was absorbed in the layout of the hall and tried to formulate a plan since there were no back exits. The watchmen in the hall had paid attention to my every move with unsmiling eyes. In minutes we would be attempting to get the last load of the luggage past two of them un-inspected. All alternative routes were eliminated.

In the elevator on my return with shoes, it dawned on me I wasn't sure the floor or the room out of which I had left. A knot emerged inadvertently in my stomach at my self-imposed predicament. Minutes earlier, my entire thought process centered on, *"How on earth are we going to get past those armed night deskmen with that much luggage?"* I remember staring at 26 floors on the elevator panel, each marked by what looked like chicken scratch. One must navigate and decipher Chinese signs with no ability to ask simple questions of our hosts. It doesn't sound that difficult of a situation, but this made simple things complicated. I lost all physical bearings.

Mentally, I retraced my steps. I muttered to myself that the CIA would fire me right now if I had been employed by them. It was futile to use the process of elimination. Every door, every hall, every number, every sign—appeared like IQ tests designed to analyze my ability to distinguish between repetitive patterns.

I stopped; I bowed my head and prayed with my whole being, "*Lord, please show me where this room is.*" My insides pleaded for some indication of direction. I don't know whether I heard the Lord, but I just moved down the hall on the floor that seemed right and I went to the room where I could hear talking and lightly knocked. Bingo! They all jumped, even though they had been expecting my immediate return. God had landed me back in the right room.

Fearing police raids, all action froze in mid-movement when I stepped into the dark room. I broke the silence. "Donna, is everything ready?" Donna looked right into my eyes as if to see if I had any second thoughts muddle me in our brief time apart. I grinned at her eagerness. Confident that we were both assured of the assignment, she recounted how many things had changed for us. "A few hours earlier we had been so disappointed when we assumed we were the only ones who didn't get to give our Bibles to the underground church. Yet that delay caused us to find the *actual* Chinese smugglers and witness what many have never heard about and can never see. God had the better plan!" she declared, letting me know God had been ordering our steps; and more importantly, to give us both confidence we were right in taking this further. The Chinese workers seemed to pick up on the significance of this moment, "*No white person* has ever gone to the underground church with our group!"

While this trip already had eradicated all boredom in my life, this experience was of a different realm. When Donna verbalized the series of events of the day leading up to this, it went beyond adventure to building my faith. This was much like a staircase with ascending levels, and to be included in the actual climactic smuggling into the interior of China was unquestionably the next step. There was no sense of being on my own. Guidance now took on a very personal dimension; it felt as if God actually took us by the hand.

The workers had the bags filled with the last of the stash of 2,000 Bibles and gave us a very young Chinese boy and lady from Hong Kong whom they referred to simply as a *connection.* She remained expressionless as they explained that she would show us where to deliver these Bibles. The pair would re-contact us once we were out of the hotel with the Bibles carried out on our person and have a taxi waiting for us.

Different sizes of luggage were placed on our shoulders and arms by the workers until the last of the Bibles were on us. Of course, by this time it is the middle of the night, and we must look very nonchalant and as natural as possible carrying these huge, heavy bags with laundry sticking out the top. Their parting words were, "Just act normal!"

Donna and I came out the door and traipsed down the hall with an obnoxious American flair—LOUD steps and inconsiderate conversation for this late hour. It just seemed to make more sense to do the opposite of what we would normally do when we were hiding something. Our journey had begun!

We swallowed hard, slowly releasing a huge exclamation of relief when we passed the hotel guards by the elevator. Their eyes bored a hole into us, but they didn't make any move to stop us. She and I had already made *our presence known on the floor* moving about like bumbling Westerners, so we continued it by yakking back and forth about absolutely nothing. We made our way downward through the elevators and were shocked to see bustling activity going on in the lobby for such wee hours in the night.

We exited through the main foyer and looked for our contact who was to be waiting for us with a cab. Much to our surprise, we waited and waited and waited for that taxi. Earlier, I had the distinct impression the Hong Kong connection looked tense when she was assigned the two Americans. *Was she afraid we would increase the danger for her? Why the wait? Was something else wrong?* Again, we waited and waited some more...

If you had driven by and taken a Kodak snapshot of the front of this hotel on July 27th, this is what you would have seen: one of the most luxuriously elegant hotels in the world with magnificent columns and carvings, gloved doormen, uniformed guards and two American girls standing out front in grand center, dressed in light day clothes lugging multiple laundry bags in the dead of night. Our lingering turned into loitering and our presence was beginning to attract attention from every direction. We mistakenly calculated that just getting out of the room unobserved, through the halls, the lobby, the elevators, and the main door would be the biggest challenge, and we would be safe once outside.

It became obvious that activity had stopped and everyone was staring at us *as if we didn't know what we were doing!* Two Chinese night watchmen abandoned their station and rapidly moved toward us. Donna mutters[48] under her breath, "Look what is coming up from behind!" Where is the taxi??? This is the first time we had been approached by guards and we prepared for questioning. To our relief, the uniformed young men did not inspect us as foreigners but were interested in the fact that we were American girls. And really, that is better than all other alternatives—to have them watch *us*, rather than the

---

[48] In the high action moments my memory relives portions of it in present tense and I preserve this quality. It is not a grammatical error.

movement of the bags. We feel like decoys in a spy movie as they joined us to make a compact circle of four.

As if on cue, Donna and I immediately initiate a performance. We stage our conflict over a watch we had purchased in Taiwan. Never had I wanted to appear so materialistic and shallow in all my life. Donna was insistent that my brother, Bill, had asked us to shop for him a silver watch and I adamantly argued he wanted the gold watch she had bought, and I desired for her to switch. The conversation was utter nonsense, but Donna and I, without any previous consultation, understood at the same moment that we needed to make a diversion. These men were quite entertained by these two American girls fighting late at night, and they kept interrupting our drama, asking us to translate various things we were disputing. We were trying to buy time as if it were a commodity on a Monopoly board. We concentrated only on each other, bantering and pushing each other's arms and hands away occasionally for emphasis, as if we were each miffed at the other for arguing. We fell into it as easily as two sisters who had been practicing this for a lifetime. The Chinese had given us our *acting* instructions: "Just act normal!" We just weren't sure how *normal* was supposed to look or how *our normal* would look to them.

We waited for what seemed like the life span of an old maid waiting for a husband—for that taxi to come for us. The men eventually shifted their attention onto our bags. They were enthralled with the amount of luggage we had. We looked down at the bulging bags at our feet as if seeing them for the first time. There they lay in all their glory with the laundry pouring out the top of each. Grabbing a shoulder strap to test the weight of our paraphernalia, the two guys indicated the bags were very BIG and heavy for laundry. They laughed at how many bags we had. It was a game of charades. Donna and I *outwardly* laughed, bemoaning how much dirty laundry could weigh. We admired their charm; we flattered their *great* strength; we monopolized their attention. As women, we make an art form out of redirecting the conversation the way we want it to go. We had much more interesting things about home, the world, our travels—*than laundry* to discuss with our *new friends!*

Surely, (what in tarnation was keeping them!!!) it is *our* taxi that is now approaching the hotel. Puzzled, the men asked if it was our cab. *How are we supposed to know which one is ours?* The driver pulls to the curb, jumps out and throws open the trunk. We see our contact motion for us. Both Chinese guards reach for our bags and we involuntarily gasp "No!" in unison and afterwards noticed it came out a little too forcefully. Then our wits came back to us...

What is wrong with us! We have always enjoyed gentlemen with manners the world over! Inwardly I deliberated, "Why should this time be any different?

It sounds *just like* God to let the '*Commies*' carry their own Bibles to the cab for us!" ...Donna nodded her unspoken agreement. Their foreheads wrinkled, revealing their confusion when they felt the enormous weight of the laundry bags—we returned their concern with animated gestures of *how strong* our helpful hosts were. I was in utter amazement that God was *using these guards* to help us transport Chinese Bibles.

Donna and I were both very accommodating when our new friends lifted them, taking care that the laundry stayed intact as we continued our incessant babbling. This is a prime reason I was delighted that Donna's gift of personality *demanded* full attention.

As we strolled toward the taxi in a dramatic *staged goodbye*, our Chinese gentlemen friends abruptly asked us, *perhaps innocently*, "Where are you going?" (Constantly on my mind was the apprehension that it only took one phone call from a civilian reporting suspicious activity for us to be followed.) Suddenly, we pretended their broken English wasn't as clear to us as it had been minutes earlier and we dodged his direct question. With great flare we profusely thanked the young men for their help as they readjusted our cargo on their shoulders. They seemed to refocus on us and revel in the attention from young female *Westerners*.

The attentive guards dramatically plopped the four heavy bags down in the trunk with a thud while the taxi driver started re-arranging our bags. Alarm!

In full view, the driver is carelessly shoving that "laundry" around in an attempt to try to close the trunk lid when the largest one topples over... [49]

From the moment those bags were put in our care, my mind had a fixation on their contents. In the time it takes to have a heart beat, I reacted. I grabbed the bag a split second before 'the contents' spilled all over the trunk interior, reset it back up with the laundry tucked around it, while Donna, like an Olympic skater in her final spins, was "performing" *extra* encores for the men. I made a note to self to recommend Donna for an Oscar when we returned to the states. Simultaneously, we open the two rear doors and plop into the backseat of the taxi, relieved that we had made our escape. Our nervous systems wanted to explode. The length of time we had been with those men was long enough that we could have procured proposals!

We notice the two dark figures in the taxi. *Our connection* sat in the middle of the narrow back seat as if she were made of stone. The boy was in the front. Donna and I resisted the urge to ask if *our connection* had encountered problems because we could not trust the driver didn't speak English. I guess we will never know why we were stranded well over an hour for her to show up in the taxi after she left the packing room.

Quickly, this Hong Kong lady instructed the driver in Chinese and he put the car in gear. Our *connection* was in deep intercession and it seemed as though her body

---

[49] Always, I relive the close encounters in present tense and again the story begs that I preserve this quality to be most faithful to the narrative.

was there, but she wasn't. The taxi drove to the downtown area. I noticed after several laps this large metropolis appeared distressingly repetitive at night. Apparently, she couldn't make up her mind where we were to be dropped because she would tell him to "pull over" and then unpredictably change her mind and we would circle. It made for some choppy sight-seeing.

As if to explain, she reminded me she was no more familiar with the city than I was. Without thinking, I had assumed, since she was chosen as our guide, she knew her way around officially and since she was Chinese, she knew her way around instinctively. If I understood her correctly she whispered that she had been *there* only once. (I don't know if she meant *once* as 'in the city' or 'to the church', but now I understood why she was so afraid.)

She spoke in a soft voice under her breath, "When I asked them, 'Where's the church?' I was told, 'Just pray, the Lord will show you!'" The person she had asked didn't know either. Now it was quite clear why she looked panicked the entire time—she was trying to hear the Lord on where to drop us off. That abruptly motivated Donna and me to do more *praying* with her, rather than merely *observing* her. Our hearts felt like they were beating loud enough for the cab driver to hear them. We had a *LOST connection!*

Our curiosity had us determined to find out what *had* happened; now we were more concerned with what *would* happen. In apparent frustration, and after much circling, she relinquished the search and issued the Chinese equivalent of, "Stop!" We all filed out and immediately went to the trunk to retrieve our bags. When the bags were safely at our feet, she motioned the taxi on. As we watched him speed away, there was no time to process the fact that we were stranded without knowing a word of Chinese in an unfamiliar foreign city, halfway across the world, left with total strangers, hauling illegal materials and now, on foot. We shouldered the four large bags while the woman and boy took the smaller ones from our hands. The city was exceptionally dark; it was not illuminated with street lamps like our cities. We were in the black of night in Communist China with the best gifts we could give strapped on our backs. Perhaps the darkness was for the best.

What still strikes me as fascinating is how much activity was occurring in their streets. I wasn't expecting crowds to be out at this time of night. I gawked at what I was seeing—these Chinese looked bizarre at night. I pondered their culture, "*What in the world were they doing out this late?*", but I guess I hadn't grasped what they were gaping at—*this very strange sight of a mixed ethnic group, mainly women, traveling at a fast rate of speed with laundry problems.*

Our connection moved us to the middle of the street. At such a quick pace we had covered quite a bit of distance when we stopped at an incredibly dark alley—the kind you would never want to enter.[50] The woman entered the alleyway and motioned for us to follow. Donna and I looked at each other, then just turned and followed. We stepped *out of* shadows *into* darkness. There were no street lamps in this dark place.

Even before our eyes adjusted we could sense we weren't the only ones in this alley. Not only was this dark place covered with people, but we were right on top of them. Old women were crouched in front of open fires and sat motionless, staring into the flames. Donna whispered, "This is like a scene you would see in some weird movie!"

People were sleeping on the ground causing us to practically trip over them. When our eyes focused, we could see people within an arm's length. It would have been helpful to have had a sign appearing which read: "*Beware: Objects are closer than they appear.*" This is a point in the trip I would like to have known more, but *the connection* and the boy had us moving at a rapid pace. **I would describe this as "the alley of a thousand eyes..."**

There was a random mixture of day and night-time activities going on openly—boys playing what looked like a regular, but very competitive, game of badminton; next to them, an old man oblivious to

---

[50] It wasn't until this year on a Monday night in the juvenile prison as I was telling about this alley my dad looked dumbfounded. Three people had warned him not to let me go to China only weeks before we left. One had described this alley to him and told him I'd be killed in this alley. All I can say is, "I am thankful for preventative prayer and a dad who let me FACE this alley."

anyone else, was taking a bath in a barrel. He didn't bother to look up at me as I stumbled over him in his bath water. In this alley, it was as though I was seeing them, but they weren't seeing me. It was an eerie place, yet we were enveloped in total peace. We were where we were supposed to be. There was no fear in us at all, *not even for a moment.*

Donna and I have so many questions about this alley. Occupied bunk beds stacked upon bunk beds lined a portion of a block. *Why were there people sleeping outside? What did they do with the beds in the rain? Why is there this much activity in the middle of the night?* The Hong Kong lady must have sensed our perplexity and explained, "These people work the three shift system." As we passed, I counted more than five beds high in the alley; beds bunked on top of each other like mattress skyscrapers. "Nothing is wasted; they use the beds like their rotating shifts. Somebody occupies each bed every eight hours," she stated.

Struggling under the weight of the bags, I remember occasionally catching myself thinking my arms were going to break off, but strength would come in waves.[51] Afterwards, we discovered we had bruises from the weight of the luggage. When our interview

---

[51] When we tried to re-enact this scene for a prison chapel, we got luggage about the same size and filled it with paperback Bibles. We couldn't lift the luggage. How had we done it that night? Was there an adrenaline rush for Bible smugglers, or angelic help? I still haven't figured that one out!

for this job had been *"Who's the strongest?"*—they weren't joking!

This alley reminds me of a tunnel ride on a rollercoaster—a suspended feeling with surreal random activity on each side, yet the ride is moving too quickly to observe the peripheral activity, right before the big drop. How we wanted to investigate the life in this place, but we only saw it for one brief flicker. **Nevertheless, we were seeing what few are able to see.**

Abruptly the alley came to a dead end and our rapid-paced journey came to a halt with three flights of steep wooden stairs, which ascended into the dim interior core of a building. This was our destination, the place we would rendezvous with another world in the kingdom of Christendom. We took a sharp turn to climb the first flight of narrow worn steps. These stairs were the most physically excruciating part of the trip, perhaps because we had nothing to distract our attention from the weight of the luggage.

The heavy door creaked as it opened when our escort pushed against it with her hand. We were ushered into this large room to face a man who was intently staring at us. *Who is he?* For a brief moment I didn't know if I should trust him, but then I grasped that he was posted as a guard to watch what was happening in the streets. I whispered to Donna, "That's why the people in the room weren't afraid when we burst through the door loaded with Bibles this late at night." This guard, which the underground church had positioned at the window facing the street, was watching our every movement through the alleys with our load as we made our way toward him. (The workers in this room stacking Bibles conveyed much less tension than the ones in the hotel.) Without hesitation and with one fluid movement, the guard lifted the straps of the heavy bags from our shoulders.

I immediately recognized the familiar face of the woman who had given me her shirt. She looked the same as when she left us—*the tears were still flowing.* She was immediately concerned, "Angie, what are you doing here? This is dangerous for you."

"Well, I just had to come see you!" I interjected, trying to lighten the mood. With a quick laugh, I added, "I wanted to personally return your shirt," as I dramatically removed the extra layer and placed it on her shoulders. She stared at me dumbfounded, "I can't believe you came." Theatrically, I grabbed her in my arms and kissed her playfully on the top of her head in celebration. She would not be consoled.

Addressing the reason for her moist eyes, I asked, "What has gone wrong?" I glanced around to see if anyone else in the room was upset.

Nodding towards a weathered faced, Chinese man, she earnestly replied, "Well, it is about the pastor; he has been in jail for 26 years now. There before us stood this man—the most humble-looking man.

"He has suffered two years of torture for refusing to quit preaching and for the love of his people. Even his family suffered, his wife died in prison for her faith in Jesus Christ. Now, he confided in me he will be returned to that prison," she informed us.

Maryann, our Chinese-speaking team member, had gathered up many remarkable facts about the plight of Chinese Christians. "He preaches five times every Sunday to overflowing crowds in this very building. The police have repeatedly warned him to stop and have jailed him regularly," she continued. Donna gasped, "*This man has been in prison longer than I've been alive!*" The thought startled my mind as I calculated her information. Mentally, I processed the length of the events of my life in terms of his years in prison and the dreadful realization of the duration of his imprisonment. I was seeing China's other side to freedom of religion.

Donna's senses were heightened with an acute awareness of not wanting to miss anything. Standing in the middle of the room she looked in every direction. "Angie, it is like there is a satisfaction in the core of my being—like being in the center of God's will and not ever wanting to leave!" She continued, "I feel completely happy, like we got the job done; but look at our lives compared to his." She nodded toward the pastor and commented, "The dedication of his life. The intensity of his life! What he's given up to spread the gospel, to fulfill the Great Commission.

And yet, these Bibles are not in the hands of the people. They still have to be moved from here. And Chinese believers are in danger every day of their lives if they are caught with a Bible. They suffer such oppression from their government!"

Maryann asked, "Would you two like to be introduced to him?" We were delighted for the chance to learn more. "Of course," we readily agreed as she motioned us toward a slender, wiry framed man across the room. She ushered us directly to him, but stepped back, paused, and made no formal introductions.

Donna let me take the lead and stood back to soak in the moment. Wasting no time on conventional formalities, I greeted him with a direct, "Hello, who are you?" He replied with much spunk, "I'm a Baptist!"

Then he shot right back at me, "And who are you?" I stated just as proudly, "I'm a Texan!"

He spoke English to our English-starved ears. Hearing someone speak your language in a sea of foreign voices was akin to hearing your favorite song come over the radio. We grasped right hands and we both broke out in simultaneous laughter. Our humor matched, and we instantly had a liking for each other. It felt like the East met the West in our handshake.

He was an agreeable man and I remember noting his eyes danced, hiding any years of personal pain. Like the impetuous impatience of youth, he had been waiting anxiously for what we had brought him. He asked me some questions. I wanted to know more about his world. His people edged me away from him, and the visit unexpectedly concluded before I was ready for our conversation to end.

My Canadian Chinese friend had made her drop of Bibles, but for some reason she had been lingering in the room. She had no idea we had been asked to come, and yet she had waited in the dead of night (which had been quite a lengthy time since we had so many delays) as if she knew we were coming. The information she gave us that night about the underground church and its challenges was invaluable. The miracle of Maryann was not only that she interpreted Chinese language for us, but she interpreted the entire underground church encounter. She personally arranged these precious moments with this pastor for me. It was like God had given us a private tour of the underground operations so *others could see it through our eyes.*

The Chinese had wanted our team to tell about the State Church, but God had brought me here to tell about the REAL Church. If we wanted a personal metaphor of a Shepherd leading sheep, God had given us a private guided tour of China so I could share what I had seen. If He had not had that English-speaking Chinese friend in this upper room—we would have dropped the bags off to nameless people, left, never to have known or understood the significance of what we were seeing. It would *merely* have been a drop-off detail in my memory instead of the opening of a *brand new world* to me.

This entire trip had made me ask, "Why was God showing me this?" God had gone to great lengths to get me here in this room. First, I was pulled out of my seat in Brownwood from a large crowd and told emphatically the Lord wanted me to go to China. Before I had time to process what the speaker had said, the audience was told that someone in the room was to pay my way. Immediately I was given a partner for the trip, which probably made me take the whole idea much more seriously. Then on the train, the guard had singled me out from everyone for my signature on that incriminating release form and the rest is history. Here we were! While our team of 240 was in bed asleep that night, we were chosen to continue on with the underground church. It seemed that I kept being whisked out of a crowd and chosen out of many to the point it was getting ridiculous. Why? Different people would answer that different ways.

~

After unloading our bags, the worker handed back our empty bags. I felt some bulk weight and checked the zipper pockets. Unlike the border inspectors, these men had missed the Bibles in the inner compartments. It was like finding hidden treasure in our bags, which were compressed, ready to be sent back to the hotel with us. *Each Bible I found felt like something particularly special,* and I enjoyed touching it. As I loaded the final few onto the table, I wondered where they would end up and who would have these very ones that were almost overlooked and left hidden in these inner pockets.

My friend explained their value: "One woman had walked *one month* to get one of the Bibles we had brought." She continued to list out the facts, "*Some had only one Bible* for the *whole* church, and there was one church who had *only one* page." (One can imagine the redundancy of the sermons in a church that only had one page.)

The shortage of Bibles in China overwhelmed us. Donna made a comparison to America's abundant supply of Bibles, "There aren't any Bibles gathering dust on coffee tables in this country! Most of us have two or three copies to spare." I agreed. When someone in our church wanted a Bible, we went to the bookstore to choose; when a Chinese Christian wanted a Bible it was a little more complicated.

~

There were two tables about the size of two double wide church social tables filled to overflowing, not with food and desserts, but with Bibles, and more Bibles. I turned around and stared, transfixed at the two heaping tables—it was something I didn't want to take my eyes off of until I had it pictured and stored in my mind. *We got all those Bibles through—every one of them!* The LORD didn't let one of them get lost.

The power of the present was intoxicating. But there was something else I couldn't put my finger on— like seeing life in layers, and I was looking at only one slice. What was it that I was wrestling with on the inside? It was like I wasn't allowed to leave, until I acknowledge *something*.

I am staring at those Bibles like I am trying to remember some specific thing. Our work was finished, the hour was late and the room of people was antsy to disperse. However, very unexpectedly, I seemed to begin to move back through time—into a hidden memory buried deep inside of me. The years seemed to be dissolving. Someone in the room abruptly interrupted this moment's passage and indicated it was important we should go, and I turned to leave.

I glanced over for one last look, and at that very moment *I had a flashback*. And the recollection came rushing back. I remembered for the first time the prayer of a nine- or ten-year old at the altar, *"God, when I grow up, I want to smuggle Bibles!"* It was like my life went into rapid rewind and paused on that one moment long ago. I saw myself at that altar.

This showed me beyond a shadow of a doubt GOD will hold you to your commitments. He will answer those crazy childhood prayers. He really listens to them. There was something about that moment that confirmed *prayer* at a level I had never known. Nothing has spoken to me as much about the power of prayer as did that flashback to a child at the altar, never-before-remembered until it forever linked to this present moment in this room. When I really think this out logically all the way through, it lets me know how seriously God takes the prayers we pray and the words we say![52]

Never had I thought about that prayer I had prayed years ago or that camp until this moment when it all came crashing back, and the memory returned, rushing over me with force. Something about those heaping piles of Bibles reignited a recollection of an agreement I had made with heaven, and God made me acutely conscious He had kept His end of our bargain. God bringing me here to this room had the air of triumph. With all the flair of a clenching signature on a contract, it was like He had delivered what He had promised. And then He waited for me to become aware of it. When I acknowledged it on the inside, I was at peace to leave.

~

Ironically, only days after being so embarrassed that I had no life story to share, He forever changed that. In this short three-day section of my life, when we were smuggling by night and acting like tourists by day, GOD totally rewrote for me my own testimony. And

---

[52] When I work with youth, I challenge them to pray bold prayers. It startled me in my own life that God remembered a prayer I had forgotten and brought it to pass. God will hold us to our commitments. If a person confesses Jesus as Lord, He holds us to it! This makes a case for youthful commitments, soldier's bargains, and jailhouse promises—God will bring your life back around to your commitment. So I dare you to take the challenge and surrender your life.

that testimony clearly gives evidence: God's plans for your life will *never be boring*.

He puts the dreams in us; He gives us our desires and then carries those desires out. Our testimony comes forth from the deepest part of our being—the area where He writes His will on our heart for our lives! Life is full of unmet desires until we step into His plans. From the moment I determined *never* to use my parents' testimony as a substitute to **the end of that very same week**, God had given me my own and I *knew* He was with me.

When I left the underground church and opened the taxi to get in, I about fell over when I saw who was sitting in the back seat. Since he[53] had a cynical view of Christians, mingling with the underground church was the last place I had expected to see him. He must have seen my surprise and explained that he had coordinated the entire smuggling operation for our team from the border crossing until now. He not only had arranged every aspect of it, he had personally continued to the final drop-off location in the heart of the city to oversee it to the finish.[54] That night in the taxi I had a question for him: "Why do you take *the personal risk* when you don't follow the Book yourself?" He answered back with much private reflection, "When I

---

[53] Name withheld because of his link to the security operation.

[54] We had had long talks on planes since we both had a hard time resting and he reluctantly admitted that he was not a believer. Late one night, he had commented I seemed different than others he had met while coordinating these trips, and questioned me as to why I believed and what I found as convincing.

watch how much these people risk in getting these Bibles, it is the *very least* I can do for them."

The taxi pulled in front of our hotel. I mused on the irony—the inception of his smuggling had begun in much the same way as I had surrendered my life.[55] I hope by now He has found a *personal* reason for taking that risk.

My mind was delirious from sleep deprivation. Still reeling from having activities in China that required both my day time hours and my night time hours—there had not been much time for any type of rest for three blurring days. Morning had come earlier than usual. A haze settled in like a thick fog covering my brain but my heart was alive and bursting. Perhaps I was delirious but the train station didn't seem very threatening today and I hoped to get some sleep while we were waiting on luggage inspections.

As the guides loaded the team on the buses with very little in our departure bags, I reflected on the part of the trip no one on the team knew anything about and I tried to process what I had witnessed first hand. Donna and I had been asked by Paul not to mention it until we were in British Hong Kong, as a safety measure for the sake of both the nationals and connections who lived under a constant security risk.

I gazed out the window as the early morning sunlight filtered into my eyes and saw hundreds of the

---

[55] As an adult, he was working for God before He knew Him, the same as I had done. (See page 32...)

elderly Chinese doing light aerobics toward the rising sun. Were they worshipping or were they collectively exercising in odd movements and rhythms? There was much I didn't know. This whirlwind encounter with China had definitely left me with some unanswered questions; however, I was fulfilled and satisfied that I had left these people in this country a gift—something that could answer *their* questions.

Departing through the same train station did not have the high-packed adrenaline surge of the first time; we were a decidedly more relaxed group than the one that had originally come through a few days prior. That station was like a ruler marking a very small but intricate measure of my life. I was forever changed by what had happened between the first time I went through that station and the second—only three short days later. Some only measured my trip by what I *carried in,* but I carried something *out* of China that had infinite value—I now had a testimony![56]

---

[56] **The last I heard of that Chinese pastor?** About seven years later, according to an article my husband found in the Dallas paper, he had been captured again. The AP report from China was made to sound as though they were handling a dangerous criminal. Fifty police officers had surrounded the pastor in the arrest. He had been put back in jail with a little notation in the paper saying he was awaiting execution.

EPILOGUE

I CHALLENGE YOU TO witness to neighbors, youth, the elderly in nursing homes, the people in prison and their children, Sunday Schools classes, international students, radio and television audiences, college students. Live life with risk and enthusiasm in your walk with God! Invite the foreigners in your community over for dinner. One of the most enjoyable evenings my husband and I had was with some college couple friends and a Hindu family who owned the hotel next to my husband's office. It was a four hour dining experience in which we had carefully prepared with special adherence to the absence of any animal products. Conversation livened up when I asked him how he sprayed for cockroaches in his hotel! Build relationships for the kingdom. Minister in pulpits, palaces and prisons... take it to the streets!

Vacations: do you use it only for your own enjoyment? Nothing makes a trip more special than having a deep conversation with a total stranger. Never go anywhere without expecting to share your testimony. As you book your tickets pray that God will seat you next to the very person whose heart He has already prepared. In Helena, Montana, I remember one young man, Elijah, who was fortunate to be seated next to me on the plane. I exclaimed as this handsome young college football player plopped down, "I couldn't wait to see who

God had for me, and you are the man!" I shared some stories from my life and he told me he was an atheist. Yet he seemed ready to talk. At the end of the flight, I explained that I was going to pray over him. He seemed slightly stunned that I planned to do it on the spot and in public. I bowed my head, "God, do something special for him that will let him know that You are there! Reveal yourself in a supernatural way in his life, today…" Making my way to my connecting flight, I was stunned when I caught sight of Elijah in the adjoining terminal in Salt Lake City, but he was even more flabbergasted than I was. He explained how he had wanted fresh flowers for his girlfriend and had looked everywhere for an airport vendor. Right in his path, he saw a fresh rose bud in new cellophane wrap, complete with an attached watering tube and vial lying on the high traffic carpet walkway with everyone stepping over it as if they couldn't see it. Picking it up, he asked those in the vicinity if anyone had dropped it. He seemed half-spooked, telling me that this happened minutes after we had prayed and parted ways. He emailed me a year later and said he wanted me to know he was actively attending church.

Use a little sandpaper on the things that are irritating about your personality and share from a genuine heart. Nothing is as attractive as a genuine twinkle in the eye. Relax and have real conversation. There are so many interesting aspects to life. Just talk. The Lord usually has a way of working Himself into the conversation!

I've seen people who are embarrassingly offensive. Do not use that as an excuse to avoid the responsibility of evangelizing. If the whole world does it wrong, YOU DO IT RIGHT! I remember I had a deep aversion to cold turkey witnessing you often have to do if you are going to talk to strangers. To be made to do tract evangelism seemed to be the death sentence. I finally realized it wasn't evangelism that bothered me but *what* I was handing out. When I improved the quality of my literature, the embarrassment went away. We purchase quality materials in bulk, and most people thank us for the book, or DVD, or for the children's Picture Bible or the CD. When you hand a person a DVD, for instance, it will keep on preaching long after you leave. I remember being in the *Tenderloin* district of San Francisco in a housing project that was loaded with drugs. The teenagers looked imprisoned in these families. A wild-eyed red headed mom asked me to help her with her fourteen-year-old teenager. I left because he refused to come to the door. When we made our rounds to the next floor, we opened a door, and I saw that same mom purchasing drugs without money from a dealer. I slipped back up to that corner room full of children and offered W.W.P.[57] movie DVDs if the

---

[57] World Wide Pictures produces movies that entertain so well that people hardly realize they are being evangelized. Crosslines College Ministry purchase such titles as *Road to Redemption, Something to Sing About, The Climb*, etc. Why spend hundreds of dollars on a mission trip for your personal travel, lodging accommodations, food, and then spend nothing on literature materials? That is going to be hard to explain on Judgment Day.

young man would come out. I will never forget the look of delight on that teenage face that I had come back for him and brought him a stack of DVDs that will keep on telling the message long after I leave.

My family missed the last shuttle from the hotel at our Nashville (NRB) Convention, and a middle-aged lady offered us a ride in her car. She was not part of our convention, just next to me in line at the concierge's desk at the Gaylord Hotel. My parents were shocked when I immediately said yes for all of us. I have found when something unusual happens, look for a door of opportunity. On the drive, this lady from California told me about her conversion to Buddhism. She was not interested in mother's testimony or mine. As we got out I tried to pay her for the ride and the gas, but she adamantly refused any compensation. I asked if she collected anything and she said "bowls". I wrote down her room number and two days later when I delivered a bowl for her collection, she was suddenly very interested in hearing about the Christian faith.

Another time, my mother switched places so I could speak with a young man in the aisle seat. When I found out he was a Christian flying home from a business trip to the Bahamas, I asked if he shared his faith with anyone on the trip? He responded, "No! but I wish I could." I gave him a copy of the notes *8 Strategies of*

(continued) I am shocked when mission teams cut costs by giving poor quality materials. The great thing about DVDs, people watch them over and over! See: www.wwp.org

Evangelism I use to train our teams. To this day he keeps in contact and supports our mission trips.

My mom was being interviewed for her book *Psalm 91* when suddenly the conversation changed directions. I was unprepared when the television cameras shifted to me and the hosts were asking me too many personal questions about smuggling into closed countries. (I had just found out they aired this program internationally.) I did not know how to answer their direct, eager questions about how to get involved. They were enthusiastic about the work we do, and I had one split second to refocus, reverse what had been said or press forward. I tried to weigh it out inside, based on prior experience—my testimony was very exciting in college groups and churches but never had I been put on the spot in an international format to announce what I do undercover.

Instead of backing away, I replied, "We are coming to your country next! Americans, I'm asking you to do the work of an evangelist when you travel or we are never going to get this harvest complete. Load your suitcases up!" Honestly, as tourists, we have much liberty in international settings, and I have found that the tourism dollar is stronger than their desire to actually stop one's freedom of speech. When you travel—prepare for the trip by ordering literature to take with you. One trick to remember in case you get busted smuggling is something I read by one of my all time favorite authors. When Corrie Ten Boom was exposed in a border crossing, customs opened her luggage and she was caught red-handed. In a moment of inspiration she reached in and began handing out books, autographing copies as gifts for their children. Culturally, it was very impolite to refuse a gift! Be bold. Be creative. Be wise as a serpent yet harmless as a dove.

Don't shortchange yourself by holding back. Common fear is never a sign that you AREN'T supposed to go. I can't tell you how many times people have told me "Don't Go!" Think of those people who took their Bibles out before the border crossing and missed the excitement when the entire team was allowed through with NO INSPECTION. Fear will trick you. They thought *God* told them *they would be caught,* and instead, they missed the excitement of being part of delivering Bibles to people who have never had one! Recognize fear for what it is.

Never forget, *God has an exciting life for you!* I stand amazed at what God did to bring this story about in my life so I could share this account with you. These are my stories, and I hope they have encouraged you. It has been an honor to take you along on our adventure. But now, it is time to put the book down and garner your own stories. The Bible tells us there is *overcoming power* in the word of our testimony...

Go get the testimony God has custom-made for your life!—and remember to pack some cotton balls!

COMMITMENT PRAYER

LORD, I PRAY THAT you will come into my heart and forgive me for all my sins. I repent for going my own way in life. I've made a decision, I want to live for you. I don't want to live a selfish life and I pray that you will take all boredom out of my life. I believe You are who the Bible says You are and that You died in my place for my sins and rose again. I confess Jesus as my Lord and I take the challenge to let You do all and anything You want with my life. Give my life purpose and meaning. It is yours. I pray that you will give me an exciting life to be used for Your service and for Your kingdom and for Your glory.

In the Name of Jesus I pray.
Amen.

www.crosslines.net

OTHER BOOKS AVAILABLE